LIGHTS OUT

LIGHTS OUT

LIVING IN A SIGHTLESS WORLD

TRAVIS FREEMAN

The Freeman Foundation
P.O. Box 2671
Corbin, KY 40702

ISBN 978-0-5781465-5-3

For information about special discounts for bulk purchases, please contact
The Freeman Foundation at 859-904-9418 or info@travisfreeman.org.

Interior designed by Caleb Seeling, http://samizdatcreative.com

Cover photo used with permission from Ocean Avenue Entertainment,
http://oceanave.tv

Cover designed by Lisa Hainline, http://lisahainline.com

Manufactured in the United States of America.

Photo credits: Unless otherwise noted, all photos are from the author's
collection.

INTRODUCTION

As the president of a university, I encounter many unique and compelling stories, but the story of Travis Freeman stands out. I was familiar with Travis's inspiring story from his days as a blind football player and outstanding student at Corbin High School in the late 1990s. However, I did not personally meet Travis until May of 2012 when I learned of his search for a teaching position at a Baptist college or university. I asked Travis to come in for an interview and subsequently offered him an adjunct position in our Missions and Ministry department here at the University of the Cumberlands. For the past four semesters, Travis has served in this position, teaching classes such as *Exploring the New Testament*, *Exploring the Old Testament*, and *Communicating Bible Truths*. Travis teaches in both our undergrad and masters level programs. He has participated in many activities on our campus, and we are excited to have him as part of our university.

I came to know Travis on a more personal level during the fall semester of 2013 as the University of the Cumberlands football team made a run at the NAIA national championship. He attended most of our home football games sitting with my wife and me as well as other members of our administration and family. Travis even traveled to the national championship game in Rome, GA to cheer on the Patriots. His attendance at these games provided me with the opportunity to talk with him in-depth and to observe him interacting with people outside the classroom. As I have observed him over the past couple of years I have become even more aware of how much he loves the University of the Cumberlands. At every opportunity Travis willingly speaks to alumni, donors and other friends of our institution, helping us promote the mission of our school. For this, I am grateful.

During this time, I also watched as my wife Dinah interacted with Travis. The two of them joked and laughed as they cheered on the Patriots to an NAIA national runner up. She loves Travis because of how he loves sports and engages people. This has made her one of his biggest fans. As a couple, we want to see Travis' story told. For this reason, we are excited about this book and the encouraging message that it represents.

I am excited about people being able to read *Lights Out: Living in a Sightless World*, because of its inspiring and compelling story. The way Travis has overcome the obstacles that he has faced should encourage all of us to do the same. He has not allowed his physical blindness to keep him from achieving his goals. From playing football, to attending the University of Kentucky, to completing a Ph.D. from The Southern Baptist Theological Seminary, at every turn Travis has defeated the barriers that stood in his way. I think we all have the tendency to assume that an individual who has a physical disability is for whatever reason unable to live a productive life. Travis' story, however, shows people that just because an individual has a disability that does not mean that the individual is incapable of living a normal, productive life. We all need to hear and heed that message.

Each of us has disabilities that we face in our lives, obstacles that we must face and overcome. We may not possess a physical disability like blindness, but we may have an emotional, spiritual, or mental issue. It could even be the day-to-day struggles we all possess. Whatever your personal disability may be, Travis' story challenges all of us to not get discouraged by it but to persevere through it. The way Travis has tackled the difficulties in his own life should serve to urge all of us to do the same. No matter what we face, we can overcome it by looking beyond our circumstances to faith in God and Christ.

When a person meets Travis, he encounters a man with the ability to put people at ease with his blindness. Because of the way Travis interacts with people in a normal and confident way, he encourages people to look beyond his disability and view him as a regular person. An encounter with Travis leaves a person changed forever because of how his life encourages people to view disabilities in a different manner.

As you read this book, I hope that Travis' life will inspire, challenge, and encourage you. I hope that you will no longer view disability as an inability, but as a mere obstacle that can be overcome. Finally, I hope that you will not be discouraged or defeated by the obstacles in your own life, but rather hopeful and confident that you can overcome those obstacles just as Travis overcame his. Now enjoy your reading of *Lights Out: Living in a Sightless World*.

Jim Taylor
President
University of the Cumberlands
Williamsburg, KY

1

BROKEN WORLD

LIFE THROUGH A CRACK IN THE EARTH'S DESERT FLOOR

I'M BLIND.

Sometimes, those two words sum up my entire identity for people, at least in their minds. Then they see a story on *The Today Show* or watch the movie *23 Blast* and their identity of me changes to four words:

The Blind Football Player.

And then, maybe, they hear about my faith or my job as a professor and I graduate to seven words:

The Christian Blind Professor Who Played Football.

At this point, the questions start coming. I listen closely to the hesitancy in the person's voice and turn toward it. (That's an important Blind Person Technique: turn toward the person who is speaking.) I hear, "But how did you play football blind?"

It's a fair question. I get it. I understand how people wonder about it even if I can't see their faces. How did I know whom to tackle? How did I know the placement of the ball? How did I know when the play began? When it started? Where the huddle had gathered?

More good questions. But I hear the questions behind the questions. How do you manage the darkness? What's it like to live with a permanent disability? How do you keep going? I hear the questions all the way back to what I think is probably the ultimate puzzling issue.

We're all living in darkness. Even the age-old text of the Bible says, "For now, we see as through a glass darkly..." Living on this side of heaven means that we walk around among darkness. There is one place on earth where darkness is the most complete, where it is the most brilliant in its ability to reveal light. That place is the desert.

We walk in a dark desert. All of us. We're all blind. We're all disabled. Each of us is born into a broken world. It's been damaged for thousands of years. Our kind broke it. All of our kind feels the pain of it. Sometimes that's with illness or disease. Sometimes it's through emotional turmoil. Sometimes it's the early, inexplicable death of someone we love. Sometimes, it's our own tendencies toward selfishness, greed, lust, gluttony, despair. And selfishness.

My darkness is literal. An illness struck my body and spiraled into a maelstrom that stole my sight. My most prominent disability has a name: blindness.

Yet this is not my only disability. None of us struggles with just one. I'm also disabled by the loss of a family member to murder, by my tendency to laziness, and by my bent toward frustration. These things cripple my best self.

We're a disabled people.

But here is the inexplicable truth that makes me open my unseeing eyes every morning and try again: Disability does not equal inability.

Disability does not equal inability.

Pay attention, broken one.

Disability does not equal inability.

We're handicapped. We're disabled. But we aren't done. We have an ability to be conduits of hope, kindness, love, joy, peace, and inspiration to a crippled world. We can be an oasis in some-one's desert. We can find our way to an oasis and, trudging into it with gasping breath, fall into the refreshing embrace of those who love despite their brokenness.

Someone brought me that inspiration by placing my hands back on a football. Now, two decades later, I still hear the question, "But how does a blind guy play football?" and I hear the questions at its core: "How did you go on despite disability? How did you rob disability of its desire to rob you? How do you keep walking in a dark desert?"

Keep reading. It's my joy to answer those questions.

During the time between oases, my petite mother suffered through difficult symptoms that we sum up today as Crohn's disease. With her jet black hair, fair skin, and sparkling green eyes, Mom is a beauty on the outside. But the adversities presented by a broken body—her approach to them—grew her beauty on the inside as well.

Forged in the fire of medical adversity, her ability to navigate the medical system and find healing enough to continue the journey grew with each misdiagnosis. Ileitis. Histoplasmosis. Irritable bowel. After a three-month hospital stay, they even said it was cancer.

Mom's beautiful resolve grew. Finally, in an ongoing effort to relieve her of the abdominal pain, surgeons removed four feet of her intestines, along with over half of her colon. She left the hospital weighing in at 93 pounds. She was just nineteen years old.

Mom tucked away the experiences and lessons and determined to get on with her life. She took a job at the First National Bank as a teller. One day a man—sandy brown hair and a tan that belied hours spent enjoying the sunshine— walked up to her station with a deposit from his employer. They smiled at each other and exchanged pleasantries while she completed the deposit for him. She watched him leave the bank, wondering for a minute more about him, then returned her attention to the work at hand. He kept coming to mind, though. The smile. The kindness in his eyes. The way he remembered to thank her and wave at the other tellers before leaving. She kept smiling whenever she thought of him.

He wondered about her as well. From that day on, each time he came to the bank, he headed to her window. Neither of them realized the collusion of the other tellers to ensure Larry could only go to Mary for his deposit. From that first day—when they saw the sparks fly and the bumbling, blushing conversation between Larry and Mary—they determined to work together and allow that connection to grow. Whenever Larry entered the bank, every teller suddenly needed a bathroom break or a quick trip to the back or a word with a colleague.

Neither Larry nor Mary minded. He asked her if she'd like to spend some time together, and on the Sunday of Memorial Day weekend, the new couple headed to Cumberland Falls. They hiked Eagle Falls and, by the end of their walk, realized they belonged together for life.

Even before they married, Mom and Dad talked about children. There was little hope she'd be able to battle both her health issues and pregnancy and Dad wanted to prevent the pain that they were certain would accompany any attempt of Mom's to carry a child. Having made their decision, Dad made an appointment with the doctor about one year into their marriage. He told the doctor he'd like a vasectomy.

The doctor looked at my healthy 25-year-old father and wondered at the reason behind the request. Dad let him know about Mom's heretofore undiagnosed intestinal issues. I can easily imagine the way Dad must have looked, sitting there, earnestly and honestly telling this doctor that he was ready to do anything to keep his bride from hurting any further.

The doctor cautioned them to hold off. He wasn't as certain as my parents had become that a pregnancy would exacerbate Mom's issues. They took the advice of the doctor.

Two and a half years into their marriage, Mom got pregnant. Turns out, pregnancy made her body get itself together. She often says that the healthiest time of her life was during her pregnancy with me—yeah, I'm just that easy to be around. (Also, I have a beachfront home in Oklahoma to sell you.) In all seriousness, though, the pregnancy triggered something in Mom's body that set things right for a time.

Mom and I sailed through the pregnancy right up until Super Bowl Sunday 1981. Mom had a pain and, while she was sure it wasn't yet time for me to come, she was equally sure she had a good excuse to make a trial run to the hospital in Lexington. It took her a while to convince Dad—long enough for her water to break, which did way more convincing than her words ever would have.

She and Dad hopped into our 1977 tan and brown Dodge Ram Charger and started the hour-and-twenty-minute drive.

Dad went pedal to the metal, taking speed limits as rules meant for people who didn't have a wife about to give birth on a busy Interstate 75. He flew into the emergency room roundabout and ran inside.

Mom's doctor happened to be in the ER, on his way to make his rounds. He was still in his suit from church. He turned toward Dad, his brown eyes growing wide, and said, "Larry? Where's Mary?"

Mary was back in the SUV, of course, where I continued to busily fight off a cord that kept wrapping itself around my neck. Guess wrestling in the dark started early for me. Twenty minutes after arriving at the hospital, I got an assist from the doctor and found my way into life on Earth.

Right smack in the middle of an oasis we call Kentucky.

Dad and Mom brought me home to Corbin and began settling into life as parents. Their lives were already full with good friends and good times before I arrived on the scene. However, one thing was missing, and both grandmothers didn't stay silent about it long.

"That baby needs to be in church," Dad's mom told my mom.

"If not for yourselves, do it for Travis," Mary's mom told my dad.

They discussed it. Dad had been raised in church and accepted Jesus as his Lord at Vacation Bible School as a boy. Since reaching adulthood, though, he'd let church participation lapse. Mom didn't have a church background, but she wanted every single best thing in the world for her boy, and she had a suspicion that the grandmothers were on to something.

They tried a few small churches in Corbin, none of which felt like home. Then, Mom suggested Central Baptist Church. Dad balked inwardly at first, unsure about attending the "big" church in town. But he woke up the next morning, and with no further discussion about the idea, both of them put on their Sunday best and drove to Central.

It has been an oasis in our family ever since.

2

LIGHTS ON

NESTLED IN THE MOUNTAINS OF EASTERN KENTUCKY, LIFE in the small town of Corbin revolves around family, church, neighborhood, and football—usually in that order. Every little boy—at least every little boy I knew—grew up with one dream: to become a Corbin Redhound, a member of the high-school football team.

After bringing me home from the hospital, nestled in a blue blanket for safety and warmth, Mom and Dad settled into what they'd later call one of the "easiest, sweetest periods of our family life." They worked hard Monday through Friday—Dad as a staff accountant at Interstate Coal Company and Mom still as a teller at the First National Bank. Come quitting time on Friday, though, they'd load all the camping gear and weekend essentials into the SUV, strap me into my brown vinyl car seat, attach the boat to the back, and head off to Laurel River Lake. On Sunday morning, we'd leave the tent and head into town to attend Central. As soon as the last "Amen" sounded, we jumped back in the SUV on the way to the lake.

By age two, I'd learned the joy of waterskiing. As I stood on the skis and felt the sunshine and water droplets hit my face, my little feet placed right in front of Dad's, I couldn't think of anything more fun or freeing. Within two years, Dad stayed at the wheel of our gold and blue boat, and I skied solo.

Sometimes I think about what the lake looked like. Deep

blue-green waters reflecting the lush trees ringing the water. Hills and cliffs rising on all sides, covered in enormous maples that went almost the entire way to the shoreline. Little campsites dotted the dirt shores. Smaller bits of color bobbed in the waves – kids in lifejackets.

I rarely had patience for that part of the lake—the lifejackets and prevention stuff. "Hold still, Travis," Mom said at least a hundred times as she applied sunscreen and snapped my lifejacket in place. All I could do was shift from foot to foot, staring at the gently lapping water and counting the seconds until I could jump in from a 20-foot cliff. The water never scared me. I loved it and wanted to spend as much time in it as possible. As I got older and developed into a good skier, I rode the knee board and loved jet skis. I felt at home in the water.

Our weeks rolled by in the rhythm of small-town security. We knew everyone in the neighborhood. They knew us. We tripped along the path of a joyful life that no one doubted would one day include Dad and Mom sitting in the stands, cheering on their Corbin Redhound boy.

Before I could even join the peewee league, though, I had to walk a few feet of desert. At age four, I began having a pain in my side. I told Mom, and she took me to Dr. Hacker in Corbin, who immediately sent me on to the doctor in Lexington. Other doctors wondered at his swift decision to send me to the city for treatment. For a little side pain? Looked like overkill to them, but it turned out to be a harbinger of years to come.

The doctors in Lexington discovered I not only had a kidney infection (not your usual 4-year-old problem), but I also have an odd-shaped kidney. It functions properly, but it is shaped like a ruler instead of a kidney. Because we Southern Baptists like to keep things as straight as possible, of course.

Mom tucked away the experience and expressed gratitude for the doctors in Lexington. I recovered easily and returned to running through the hills of our neighborhood and playing with my friends Matt and Staci as we rolled Tonka trucks all over and reveled in the sandbox in my backyard.

The action lived outdoors for me. I never, ever wanted to be inside. With so much to do, to see, to run through and to, I didn't want to be contained within four walls.

Eventually, during my third or fourth grade year, I got a taste of being a Corbin Redhound. As water boy, I proudly ferried water to the high school team, watching them from the sideline and dreaming of the day I'd be on that field in that jersey. The day lay like a promise on the horizon. I could taste it.

For as long as I can remember, I have loved going to church. It's a place of friendship and life and family. Royal Ambassadors, Bible drills, and Vacation Bible School gave me fun ways to fulfill my desire to learn about the Bible while not giving up the fun or adventure.. How did this book—written thousands of years ago—apply to me? I couldn't get enough of it. I never have gotten over it. There is something mysterious and powerful, deep and unplumbed, within the pages of a Bible.

The summer after fifth grade, I headed off to Laurel Lake Baptist Camp. Four years earlier, I had walked the aisle and been baptized, but my faith was not my own yet. Instead of a personal choice, it felt like something I should do, so I did it. Becoming a Christian just stood as the next step in my life. But at Laurel Lake Baptist camp, I experienced the conviction of sin for the first time. As I sat in worship service on the last night, listening to the gift that a perfect God gives to have relationship with us imperfect humans, I truly came to the understanding that I was a sinner in need of a savior. I knew that my sinful and broken state separated me from God and that my only hope for reconciliation with him—for life—was Christ. When I realized my feet walked a dark desert floor, I finally looked up and saw the brilliance of the sky above, created by One who could get me from here to Him.

On a Thursday night in July, 1992, I came under the conviction of sin, repented of that sin, and became a faithful follower of Christ.

Life would be a bit different now that my internal, spiritual Light switched on. Not drastically different from the outside—I'd still go to church and all and hadn't exactly been living a hellion's life before—but my reasons for going would be changed. Now my life had the motivation of loving this Jesus who'd died on a cross for me and rose again, conquering death, bringing Life and Light to all who accepted Him. I thought about that. What would I need to do now? How would life alter in a way that allowed me to get to know Him more?

For anyone growing up in a Baptist church, the answer is obvious: read the Bible, or what we called "getting into The Word." Read His words, study His ways. Let His wisdom become the light by which we walk.

But when? Every morning, I got up, dressed, and headed off to school. After school, my day continued with football or basketball practice. Afterward, I came home, dumped my backpack, and headed outside to join Matt and Staci or other friends playing. None of that seemed like an activity to discontinue.

I considered the situation and came up with the only solution that seemed to work. I'd need Mom's help.

Awaking one morning as usual to the sound of Mom's voice and her touch on my shoulder, I grabbed the opportunity. "Mom, I need a favor."

"Okay. What?"

"I need an alarm clock."

Mom looked at me quizzically. "An alarm clock?"

"I need to read the Bible more, and the only time I can think to do it is in the morning. So, I'm going to get up an hour earlier."

To me as an adult, knowing what would hit me a year later, that memory holds fresh and deep meaning. I was about to spend an entire year rising early, reading the Word, and praying. A year before the hardest time of our little family's life would commence.

A year in an oasis, drinking from the Fountain of Life, letting its refreshing waters gush over me. I'd be drenched. Soaked.

This isn't surprising. God always prepares us for the bumps in the path ahead. Moses had his time in Egypt. Mary and Joseph had their time in Egypt as well. Noah had the phase of building the ark. Numerous people today talk about the months and years before their hardship being a time of preparation. God doesn't tempt us, of course, but I know He allows us to pass through the fiery desert expanse between oases. Without that process, we can't be refined. And who wants to sit around as a dirty lump of nothing useful or edifying when he can instead be transformed into a substance of recognizable value?

So for a year, I rose an hour early each morning, read the Word, and prayed. I stood in the current of the Living Water. Without that year, the remainder of this story would be very, very different.

3

LIGHTS FLICKERING

MID-JUNE. FAT, FULL LEAVES FILLED THE OAKS AND MAPLES climbing on our mountains. My bare feet sank into lush grass as Matt, Staci, and I ran all over the neighborhood. We'd been cooped up in classrooms for far too long; now, finally, the freedom of summer break seeped into our bones. My first year of middle school flashed in the rearview; truth be told, it presented a fairly decent image.

I'd begun to taste "real" sports – playing Optimist league football for the Greenwaves and Optimist league basketball. Pretty soon, I'd become a middle-school football player for the Redhounds.

Life rocked.

And the future held nothing but promise.

My bags sat by the bedroom doorway, packed and ready for a brand new camp.

Away from home.

Camp Bethel Ministries in Wise, Virginia is every twelve-year-old kid's dream. A shallow, muddy creek running between two green banks, its waters the color of chocolate milk. Tires and logs cutting through or over the muck at regular intervals provide tests for kids to prove their mettle. Archery. Human bowling. Slip and slides. A lake, complete with a rope swing that let any brave kid sail through the air for a split second before gravity took over and landed him in the water. Sermons and music that sounded interesting and applicable to my twelve-year-old self. Knot-tying. Throwing axes at enormous pieces of wood. Shooting. Basketball. Kickball. Canoeing. Paddle-boating. Volleyball in the sand.

I loved every single second of it.

The lights were on and blazing in my life. Every day brought a new adventure. A ropes course to tackle. A wall to climb. A laugh to enjoy and an experience to have. Each night, I fell into bed, slept hard, dreamt of the football glory to come in the fall, and woke up ready to do it all again the next day.

I returned home on Saturday.

By Wednesday, my headache began.

Wednesday

Suddenly, shards of darkness splintered through the bright lights of life. Explosions of pain sent shrapnel flying through my mind. Mom came home from work to find me lying on the couch in a darkened living room, trying hard to not move my head. She and Dad stuffed me full of headache medicines – feeble shields against the onslaught behind my eyes.

I probably just needed some rest from the whirlwind of camp activity. A deluge of outdoor fun—even for a kid who rarely sat still—should be followed by time to get your bearings. Late nights and early mornings will have their way, whether a boy acknowledges it or not. I needed rest.

At least, that's what I hoped. Mom wondered otherwise, called the doctor, and made an appointment for the next day.

But my good intentions of recovering flew out the window, set in flight by an invitation from Uncle Durk and Aunt Sandra to come swim. Sleep could wait another day. What kid says no to swimming? Not this one.

I pulled on my suit and trudged to the car, pushing my feet

forward despite the pounding waves in my head. The sight of the sun-dappled water beckoned me. My spirit willed it well – but my flesh roared back its negation.

I meagerly sat on the chaise lounge. As I leaned over into a prone position, I closed my eyes against the promise of the water and pulled a towel over my head.

Tomorrow. I'll feel better tomorrow. Just need to rest.

Thursday

On Thursday, my headache and I walked slowly to my grandmother's while Mom and Dad went to work. The walk felt miles longer than it should, each step dogged by the glaring summer sun overhead. I finally arrived at my grandmother's front door and escaped into the shaded sanctuary of her living room. She could tell I didn't feel well and offered me all manner of grandmotherly love—hugs, cookies, TV time. All I wanted, though, was to lay on the stillness and quiet of her couch.

Mom found me on that couch when she arrived after work. Alarm sizzled down her spine. What was this? Travis, lying down, in the middle of the day? First the poolside, towel-covered incident and now this. She listened to my grandmother tell her about the quietest, stillest day of my life as she glanced back and forth from Mamaw to me. Comprehension of the scene before her wouldn't come. One day down, okay. But two days? In a row?

She placed her cool hand on my forehead. Nothing but skin met her inquiring touch. No fever. No tell-tale clamminess. Her motherly instinct rose up and demanded medical attention.

Mom bustled me out to the car, shielding my gaze from the still-scorching sun as she reclined the seat. She pointed our vehicle toward the local doctor's office.

I didn't feel like going to the doctor. I felt like lying in bed very still with all the lights off. The fun and adventure I'd enjoyed just a couple days prior seemed very far away now. Jumping in a lake and flying on a rope swing felt worlds away, painful even to picture in my mind's eye.

I pushed against the fear that welled up each time I wondered: what could cause this kind of pain in just two days?

We entered the doctor's office, and Mom marched toward the receptionist's window. I blocked out the sound and lights as much as I could, wanting only to get to the doctor, find out the problem, and fix it. A nurse opened the door and called my name—too loud! —and we stood. The nurse guided us to an exam room, and I obediently climbed up on the paper-covered table.

The doctor entered. He prodded my neck, checked my ears, looked in my throat, and asked me some questions.

I mumbled answers.

He asked Mom questions.

She answered, though I didn't listen.

A few words came from the doctor.

Many came from Mom.

"You're just an overprotective parent," I heard him say.

I wanted to scream, "My mom is not overprotective!" I wanted to tell him about how she let me ski solo at four and run all over our neighborhood by myself and with friends and how she let me go off to camp just a week ago.

I didn't speak, though. Speaking shattered what meager peace still existed behind my eyes.

We quietly, slowly drove home. I walked into the house, careful to keep my head as straight and level as possible, and lay down gingerly on my bed. Mom doped me up with Tylenol, and I pushed away the fear again.

What beast had invaded my brain? When? How? What allowed it? What would remove it? I'd never hurt like this.

I kept my eyes closed and asked God for sleep.

Friday

When I woke on Friday, the internal bombs felt more like firecrackers, so Mom dropped me off at my grandmother's again and drove to work. Memaw mothered over me as she'd done the day before. My desire to play warred with my worry that if I did, I'd set off the mental landmines again.

The day passed with no new explosions. Mom returned to find me up and about, if somewhat subdued. Encouraged by any evidence of my returning health, she announced we were going to the movies. *Jurassic Park*!

As we entered the darkened theater with Snickers and Butterfingers in hand, I buried the residual fear and resolved to focus on the coming entertainment. Camp hangover. Had to be. Not worth another thought, I told myself. Too much sun. That could be it. I settled into the comfy padded seat and prepared to be amazed. Mom offered me the candy, but—for the first time ever—I didn't really want it.

I ignored her worried look to focus on the screen. Loud, thumping noises reverberated through the theatre. I stared at the pitch-black screen. Red words faded into being—JURASSIC PARK—and out again.

Insects buzzed. The black faded once more to reveal tall stalks of a plant at night. Flash on the face of a concerned man in an orange hardhat. Skip back to the palm tree swaying against the moonlight of a dark sky. Thunder rumbled. More concerned men in their orange hardhats.

Zoom in on a man in a fedora wielding a serious-looking silver shotgun. Back to the palm trees where now it's apparent that something huge is on the move behind them. An enormous *thing*.

A cage is brought in on a forklift. Men yell instructions all around. The thing in the cage snorts. Growls. Squeals. Heavy. Foreboding. Fedora man urges the hardhat men to go once more toward the cage. They obey, pushing the crate up against a gate. Fedora man commands, "Open the gate!"

The thing suddenly pushes its crate back from the gate. A hardhat man is dragged halfway inside the cage. That thing has the human! The music crescendos, shrieking danger.

Fedora man dashes forward, holding onto hardhat man. He throws himself into the tug of war while yelling for the remaining hardhat men to, "Shoot her! Shoot her!"

Fade off to a scene of tranquil water.

A man doesn't forget the last movie he'll ever see.

Anyone who has watched *Jurassic Park* knows that the grand idea doesn't turn out very grand. I hung on through every twist and turn in the jungle. Each time a dinosaur foot pounded down, I heard it. Each screech of a pterodactyl seared through my brain. Every single scream of, "Help!" or, "Run!" caught my ears and glued my eyes to the screen. I didn't turn away. I hung in until that helicopter flew away with the survivors and we panned out over the gently rolling waters to watch a flock of seagulls soaring along.

Then I gave in and turned to Mom.

"My headache's back."

Saturday

Saturday morning, as soon as we woke, Mom called our local doctor again.

"Travis' headache still hasn't gone away," she told the nurse. "It's been four days and it's getting worse. I really think he needs to be seen again."

"Give him some Tylenol," they said. "He'll be all right. It's to be expected with a boy his age, approaching puberty."

Mom hung up with a huff I could hear clear to my bedroom. Worry invaded my mind again. I told it to hush.

Sunday

Sunday morning dawned and we trudged to church. The chore of getting dressed—thinking through what I would even wear—felt insurmountable. I ended up wearing the first thing my hands touched. Who cared if it didn't match? Surely a lifetime of matching Sundays would make up for this one.

We entered church, and I wanted to hang out with my friends. I wanted to care about the words coming from their mouths, but the pounding behind my eyes wouldn't allow it. The pews loomed before me as makeshift beds, a welcome sanctuary.

For the first time in a while, I settled into Mom's side and stayed there through the service. Her warmth and the hush of a holy gathering created a cocoon into which I willingly fell. At the final, "Amen," Mom, Dad, and I avoided our usual routine of sticking around to catch up with folks. No desire for after-church lunch or get-together existed.

We arrived back home, and I fell into the dark safety of bed.

I think Mom and Dad would have skipped service later that night—very uncharacteristic of us—except for my determination to attend. While I hadn't been able to practice with the children's choir due to camp and my ongoing headache, I didn't want to miss the chance to support my friends as they sang. The headache would end at some point, and I didn't want to be left with the disappointment of having missed their performance.

So at 7 p.m., I put on my green shorts and burnt orange shirt, and we once again drove down the hill to the church.

I didn't make it through the performance.

The sound, the lights, and the noise of the crowd combined into one giant sledgehammer intent on banging my brain out of my skull. I stumbled out the door and down the hallway, just trying to get away. I looked up and saw Mom coming toward me. I buried my head in her shoulder and bawled, hoping the pain would escape with the tears.

Mom grabbed Dad and hustled us to the car. Baptist Regional Medical Center Emergency Room, here we come.

I got some relief at the ER that night. A shot of Demerol can have that effect. But Demerol washes out like the tide at night, and when it did, the headache crashed on the shores of my mind. I couldn't spend the rest of my life on Demerol. We needed someone to determine the *cause* of the headache.

While the drug dripped its waves of ease into my veins, Mom and Dad talked with the doctor.

No cause could be identified. I demonstrated migraine symptoms, so I received a diagnosis of a migraine and treatment for such.

With the pain back out to sea, we returned to the oasis of home and hoped Monday would find me miraculously cured.

It didn't.

Monday

Mom called the local pediatrician on Monday, explaining that I'd now had a migraine for five days and she felt fairly certain that shouldn't be chalked up to puberty or treated with Tylenol. I listened to the worry lacing her voice as she let the nurse know of our ER run the night before. Could we get a referral to a specialist in Lexington?

She was denied.

I have the advantage now of knowing what's coming. In the early years of aftermath, I wondered sometimes if—at any point in my headache saga—someone had made a decision to look further for a cause, my life would have turned out differently. It's easy to get lost in the darkness of what-if because it holds an illusion of control. It places responsibility for outcome in the hands of humans. It lets us think that we can take an action and expect a given reaction.

We don't live in that kind of world. I can step off the roof of a building. I very well may hit the ground and be road pizza. Or, at just the time I step off, an enormous gust of wind could come and push me back onto the rooftop. Or someone else could have entered the roof at just that time, saw and comprehended my plan, and jerked me back to safety. Or. Or. Or. If. If. If.

The space between oases is riddled with cracks. We all fall through them at one time or another. How far we fall and what we land on gives us our stories.

Turns out I have two parents who don't tend to take no for an answer from a doctor who is ignoring parental concern. Just as Mom hung through her desert to a diagnosis as a teenager, she'd see me through this journey somehow. If a way existed, she and Dad would find it. Isn't that how they'd gotten me in the first place?

When Mom called Dad at work on Monday to say our local doctor saw no reason to refer me to Lexington, Dad took a little walk.

Right into the insurance office at his company.

Debbie Baceleri greeted him and invited him into her office. He sat and explained to her what I'd been experiencing. As he shared the ongoing saga, Debbie's forehead creased. She grew still. She didn't blink.

Dad finished. "And so we can't get a referral to Lexington, and we're not sure what else to do."

Debbie sat up straight and reached for her phone. This didn't sound right. She dialed Marna, their on-staff nurse, and asked

Marna to join her and Dad in the office.

Dark-haired Marna arrived, and Dad began the story anew. She crossed her arms, leaning on the desk and staring intently as Dad shared his concern that his boy—previously never still— now lay on the couch in darkened rooms holding his head.

Marna looked through her glasses at Dad and back to Debbie. "He needs to see a doctor in Lexington."

Debbie agreed, picked up the phone again, and called Dr. Robinson's office in Lexington.

Dr. Robinson was on vacation, so Debbie arranged an appointment with Dr. Blake for the very next day. Dad thanked Debbie profusely—hope! —and arrived home to triumphantly give Mom and me the good news.

Debbie and Marna—stars in the desert's night sky.

Tuesday

On Tuesday, Dad left work early to join Mom (who got off at 2 p.m.) in taking me to Lexington. Misery had invaded my world so insidiously, I hardly cared who we saw, only that some-one tell us the problem and fix it. I couldn't eat. I couldn't sleep. It hurt to open my eyes. The pain cascaded through every facet of my mind. Everything I did made it hurt worse. Movement. Thinking. Breathing.

I whiled away the hours, reminding myself of the hope that lay on the horizon. Just over the hill of this stretch of desert lay the promise of a doctor's appointment. Surely, surely we would be granted the refreshing experience of an answer.

As the sun began its descent, we piled into our 1987 gold Celebrity and hit the road for the hour-and-a-half drive to Lex-ington. We were to be Dr. Blake's last appointment of the day. I lay in the backseat, breathing with purpose, counting breaths and guesstimating how many more I could take between here and the doctor. I needed to throw up, but I didn't want to because I just knew it'd make my head hurt worse.

Internally giving up the battle, I sat up and leaned into the front seat to ask Dad to pull over so I could puke.

I never got the words out.

Somehow I threw up into the front seat and did not get any on my parents, but I filled the space between them. We pulled over anyway, and Mom managed to clean off the seat as best she could while murmuring repeatedly, "It's okay, Travis. It'll all be fine." She cared less about being clean and more about getting to the doctor before he left for the day. We rolled down the windows to whisk away the stench and motored on toward the Lexington Clinic.

As soon as we met Dr. Blake, a sense of relief swept through our anxious little clan. He came into the little exam room, filling up the rest of the available space. He sat down and looked at me first. Just looked. Then, as he checked my glands and gave me a thorough exam, he said, "Tell me what's been going on with Travis."

Dr. Blake kept up a running list of questions and conversation with Mom and Dad. When did I eat last? When did this start? Did it get worse at certain times of the day? Did it ever go away? Had I wrestled with migraines in the past? What had I been doing when it started? Were there changes to my usual behavior?

Dad and Mom unloaded the whole story. How I'd been fine at camp, then woke up with a headache on Wednesday that hadn't gone away, only wavered between bad and horrible. About calling the doctor, then going to the doctor, and being mostly dismissed.

When he heard that little tidbit, his hands stilled on my neck and he turned toward Mom. "They said what?"

Mom clarified that we'd basically been dismissed.

He couldn't believe a pediatrician had blown us off.

I wanted to smile—finally, someone slowing down, looking at me, and seeing that something had gone off the rails in my body. Smiling, though, meant using my head and face, so I smiled inside instead.

Dr. Blake kept poking and prodding, questioning and clarifying. Finally, he sat back and sighed. "I think it's just a headache. I don't see anything else wrong right now."

My heart sank. *No. You have to tell us why.*

Dr. Blake picked up on the despair that renewed its hover around us.

"Happily," he said, "we can get rid of a headache."

I was taken to another room, this one with a hospital bed. The IV needle barely hurt compared to my head. Soon, the bliss of Demerol again dripped through the tube and into my veins. Liquid relief poured into my desert. I refused to acknowledge that it would dry up before the pain did.

Dr. Blake gave Mom a prescription for steroids. Once the narcotic had fully escaped from the IV bag to my body, we left.

I felt good. Okay, that's probably a given since Demerol now danced through my bloodstream. But as bad as I'd been hurting when we walked in, the sudden lack of pain had me bouncing back into regular life. I asked if we could make a stop before home and, within minutes, walked through the doors of Sports Unlimited, where I picked out an Iron Man sports watch and dared to dream about football again.

Half of summer lay behind me already. I'd be a Corbin Redhound soon! Mom and Dad, thrilled to see me taking an interest in life again, decided to extend our visit a little further with a visit to the Fifth Quarter for dinner. My stomach still felt unsettled, so I didn't eat much, but hope that I'd finally escaped the suffocation of pain had me grinning ear to ear nearly the entire ride home.

Wednesday morning, the headache returned with a vengeance.

Wednesday

See, that's the thing about pain. We can mask it for a while, but if we don't get to the root of it, it's going to come back. And when it does, we're going to spiral back into that hopelessness of knowing we have no control and no real knowledge of what we're dealing with.

When I opened my eyes Wednesday morning and felt the blinding pain sear across my forehead and behind my eyes, a shot of dread closely followed it. I stared at the Troy Aikman, Reggie White, and UK basketball posters on my walls as long as I could. I tried to will away the pain. To place myself back in the pain-free zone of the night before.

I didn't want to tell Mom and Dad. I wanted it to be over. I didn't like worrying them, and I didn't like worrying myself. The summer kept slipping away and here I lay, just waiting on pain to leave.

But it hadn't. For seven days. An entire week of pain. It hadn't left. It had set up camp. Would it ever let me go?

Not by me ignoring it.

"Mom!" I called out, squinting at the volume of my own voice.

Mom appeared in my doorway. "Yeah, Travis?"

"My headache's back."

Handling relationships can be a delicate thing in any situation. Add to the experience that you live in a small town where today's slight is tomorrow's blown-out-of-proportion story at the beauty salon, and it's a little easier to understand why Mom took the next step she did.

She did *not* call Dr. Blake in Lexington.

She called our local pediatrician again. Surely, once our local doctor heard of Dr. Blake's attention to the situation, she'd get off the "overprotective mom" list and be heard.

Mom relayed all that had happened in Lexington, ending with, "And now his headache is back and he's running a low-grade fever."

"What is his fever?"

"99.2."

"Well, we really don't consider that a fever."

It seemed my crack in the desert would widen before we found a way out.

Thursday

The next day, with the headache still in force but my fever unchanged, Mom called Dr. Blake.

"Bring him back up here," he said.

So, back into our little gold Celebrity. Back along the interstate. Back into the Lexington Clinic. Back into Dr. B's little exam room.

The lackadaisical approach of our local doctor lay dormant in the dust. Dr. B threw the force of his renewed attention at me, determined to ferret out the cause of my suffering. He ordered a spinal tap. The nurses laid me on an exam table in the fetal position and then numbed the area around my spine in the middle of my back.

"It's so important that you don't move, Travis," the nurse said. "You hear what I'm saying?"

"Yes, ma'am."

The nurse looked at Mom and Dad. "If he moves during the procedure, he could end up paralyzed."

Did she think I couldn't hear her? I squinted and focused hard on the black of my eyelids. *Don't move. Don't move. Don't move.*

A shooting pain pierced my back. *Don't move! Don't move! Don't move!*

"Breathe, honey," the nurse advised me. "Easy."

I didn't want to breathe. I wanted it to be over. Breathing meant moving. Breathe and risk being paralyzed? No, thank you. Terror flooded my system. I gritted my teeth and pictured the football field, the lake, the church—anything to keep from crying out as the needle entered my spinal column. *Don't sneeze,* I thought. *Just be still and hang on.*

I held my breath as long as I could, squeezing Mom's hand and praying for it to be over. I felt the needle leave my spine.

"All done," the nurse told Mom. "You've got a brave boy here,"

Mom agreed. "I know it."

The spinal tap revealed that my white blood count had risen a bit over normal. Combined with the headaches, Dr. B suspected I'd begun the end of a battle with viral meningitis. He told my parents, "If his temperature is 100, I'll put him in the hospital and do more tests."

My temperature sat at 99.3.

Dr. B gave me another IV of Demerol and—with nothing left to do—sent me home. Before leaving, he told my parents, "If his temperature reaches 100, I'll put him in the hospital."

We left with not only a possible diagnosis, but also a plan of action if things continued to head south. I rested in those small victories.

We'd barely been home an hour when Dr. B called to check on me.

Mom said, "His fever is still just under 100."

At home I'd stay.

While the earth around us cracked in myriad directions, we did our best to keep a firm footing. Though my heart and hopes were firmly planted on the gridiron, I was also a little boy growing up in Kentucky and the time of year had come to do what all little boys in Kentucky do.

Dad and I parked ourselves on couches – him sitting, me lying down with eyes half closed against the TV glare – and watched the NBA draft to see which Kentucky Wildcat landed with which team.

Congratulations, Jamal Mashburn.

The drone of the overhead fan crept beneath my slumbering mind and whirred it awake. I desperately wanted it off. I stared through the gloom at it, contemplating the thought of lifting my head and reaching for the cord. Not worth the added pain. I called out for Dad.

"Yeah, Travis?" he asked from my doorway.

"Could you turn off my fan?"

"Sure." Dad walked into my room and reached up for the cord that controlled the fan speed. Inadvertently grabbing the other chain hanging from the fixture, he pulled. Bright light flooded the room, a sudden glaring sun in the darkness.

My hand flew up to protect my eyes. Too much force.

I hit my left eye hard and cried out as pain exploded not only in my face, but also behind my eye.

"Travis! Are you okay?"

"Yeah, yeah." I assured Dad as best I could, with bowling balls knocking together behind my eye. I settled back in and tried to go to sleep.

Friday

I woke up Friday morning to the sound of Mom's voice.

"Travis? Travis. Wake up, honey."

I opened my eyes, already squinting against the coming pain.

Except it wasn't there.

No pain.

None.

At all.

FINALLY! I could get back to life! Dr. B must have gotten it right. A nasty bout with viral meningitis that had finally reached its end.

"Mom, my head doesn't hurt!" I spoke at top volume . . . because I could!

"At all?" she asked, the cordless still in her hand where Dr. B – who'd called to check on me – waited.

"At all."

Mom reported the good news to Dr. B while I bounded out of bed.

He told her, "I really feel like this is over."

We did, too, and breathed a sigh of relief.

I went to the bathroom and stared at my eye in the mirror. Should I tell them that it hurt? I debated internally. We'd all had enough of me being in pain. I didn't want any more doctor time. Precious little remained of the summer, and no doubt Mom would have me sitting in an eye doctor's office if I told her my eye hurt.

Except, well, it *hurt*. I entered the kitchen for breakfast and sighed. "Hey, guys, my eye really hurts."

Dad told Mom about the incident with the fan.

"How bad is it?"

"Not too bad."

"Okay, if it still hurts this afternoon, we'll go the eye doctor."

Good enough for me. I wanted this ordeal over and done. I wanted normalcy and typical summer mornings back. We finished up breakfast, Mom and Dad returned to work and I set off across the yards of Kentucky grass to Mamaw's for the day.

Having been out of commission for over a week, I eagerly anticipated the return to a real summer experience hanging out with Matt and Staci.

Mamaw, though, had other plans. Her worry had only built since watching me lie quietly on her couch. "I think you should take it easy today, Travis," she told me. "We don't want to do too much too soon with you gallivanting all over the neighborhood and have that headache come back."

Hindsight allows the wisdom of her words to ring crystal clear. I stayed indoors with her most of the day. Truth be told, I agreed with her a little. I didn't want to do anything to bring back the kind of pain I'd been in for a week.

My eye hurt and, if I looked at it long enough, I could tell it had puffed up some. I decided not to look at it too long. I wanted very badly to be well.

When Mom came to pick me up that afternoon, she stared at my eye. "Does it still hurt?" she asked. "It's very swollen."

"Yeah, it hurts. I'm sure it's fine, though," I replied. "Just dumb me, whacking myself in the eye."

Neither Mom nor I saw any connection between my swollen eye and my headaches. I'd awakened headache-free, she'd had a whole day at work, and only now had gotten a good look at an eye that had spent the day swelling.

Still, it's probably pretty obvious by now that Mom's vigilant about health. She took me to Dr. McClintock, our family eye doctor, to make sure I hadn't done any significant damage.

Dr. McClintock, with his thin brown hair, khakis, and button-up shirt, is a methodical and certain man. He knows his business and he likes helping. He asked Mom what had happened and Mom—only now realizing there might be a connection—told him the whole story of the past nine days. The headaches, trips to Lexington, and how I'd at last awakened *without* a headache just this morning but *with* a sore eye from bonking myself in the head.

He examined my eye to see if I had a detached retina or some other new disaster, but found nothing. "Put ice on it," he advised Mom. "It should be better by the morning. If it isn't, give me a call."

We gathered in the family room that night for a family meeting. A decision needed to be made. While I'd been lying in my bedroom for nine days, Mom and Dad had been praying not only about my condition, but also about their response to it. Mom needed to leave the next morning for the Myrtle Beach mission trip with our youth group from church. She'd already told them she couldn't go with me in pain, but now my pain was gone. Should she go?

I'd eaten meals all day and kept them down. Aside from a swollen eye, I felt fine. Normal, even. I voted for her to go. Dad joined with me.

Mom—not having done a single bit of prepping until this point—flew into a flurry of shopping and packing.

Saturday

Wearing her purple-and-orange "Prayer Warrior" t-shirt, Mom crept into my room before the sun and kissed me goodbye.

I woke up enough to say, "Mom, be sure you bring me something back."

She promised.

Dad took her to the church to join up with the youth group.

Mom kissed Dad goodbye and said, "I'll call you at the first stop to make sure Travis is okay." These were the days before cell phones and constant communication.

At 6 a.m., Mom and the youth group rolled out of the parking lot toward Myrtle Beach.

Dad returned to the house to find me sitting in the recliner with an eye that kind of looked like Muhammad Ali had done a number on it. Far from being better in a day, it had gotten worse.

Dad called Dr. McClintock with the update.

"Meet me at the office at 9," he responded.

This time, Dr. McClintock shone a light deep into my eyes.

He gasped.

"We have to get him to UK Hospital. Immediately."

4

LIGHTS DIMMING

MY FATHER WOULDN'T CALL HIMSELF A FAST THINKER. Neither would his family. He likes to mull over his decisions, weighing all the options, until Mom and I feel crazy. Decide already!

But in that moment, Dad knew exactly what to do.

The urgency from Dr. McClintock told Dad three things: (1) something lurked behind my eyes that sparked an immediate need for help, (2) he couldn't wait until Mom checked in from the road before he decided what to do, and (3) he shouldn't drive me to Lexington alone. What if something happened on the way?

He needed help.

Dad called Aunt Helen, my mom's sister, and quickly explained the dire turn in my situation. In no time at all, Aunt Helen arrived with her state-trooper husband Eddie. With Eddie at the wheel of their red Pontiac Grand Am, we flew down the interstate as Dr. McClintock called a colleague, Dr. Conklin, to meet us at the ER.

We didn't wait long at the ER. Dr. Conklin, still in his weekend shorts and flip-flops, greeted us on arrival, and the nurses began taking my vitals with a disciplined intensity. My fever had climbed to 103.5. Dr. Conklin looked deeply into my eyes and saw what had alarmed Dr. McClintock so severely—an infection not just homesteading behind my eyes, but now furiously dividing, growing, and gobbling up more and more room like a demented Pac Man.

My other eye swelled up. The infection intended to take every inch of ground available.

Were the doctors staring at bacterial meningitis? A virus? Some other infection? Nobody knew for sure.

A nurse attempted to insert an IV into my arm, but my nine-day headache hadn't allowed for much eating or drinking, and dehydration is not a friend to the veins. My pathways had shriveled to nothing during my time in the desert. She tried over and over to find a vein in my arm.

A needle pierced the bend of my arm, jabbing under the skin, rolling over and around my puny veins. I watched at first, hoping my own force of will could guide the sharp point to its intended destination. After the fifth attempt, I had to look away. Jab. Dig around. Roll. Jab. Dig around. Roll.

"I'm sorry, sweetie," the nurse kept saying. "Hang in there. I'm sorry." Jab. Dig around. Roll.

"Let's try the foot," she said softly.

I felt hands on my foot, pulling my leg straight. Severely in need of fluids, my muscles rebelled and cramped up. Before she could get a needle in, the muscles in the arch cramped. I cried out. "Wait! Stop!"

"It's okay, sweetie," she kept murmuring. "Almost there. I'm so sorry."

She couldn't hear my words over her own. "My foot! That hurts!"

"I know, honey, it'll all be over in a second."

Dad stepped toward the bed and grabbed my hand. "Trav—

"Cramp, Dad!"

Dad caught on to the real cause of my pain. "Wait! His

foot's cramping!"

The nurses immediately release my foot, which stayed bowed in an arch.

"Oh my goodness!" A medical technician began rubbing the muscle back into its relaxed position. As the muscle released, I eased back into the bed.

"Thanks, Dad."

"I love you, Trav."

While the tech made certain my foot stayed in a neutral position, the nurse returned to my arm. "Let's try one more time." I didn't know if she spoke to me or to herself.

This time, the needle found its mark. She breathed heavily and secured it with a piece of tape. Patting my arm, she leaned down closer to my face. "Such a brave, brave boy. Good job."

"Thank you," I said.

With a line running into my body, the tests could start *en masse*. First up, another spinal tap. Was this bacterial meningitis instead of the previously diagnosed viral meningitis? Bacterial meningitis is the dangerous kind. It will kill if not addressed in the early stages.

My white blood cell count scored at 30,000. The normal level is 4,500-10,000. Clearly, *something* had launched an attack, and my immune system spun into warp speed to fight it. They kept coming with the tests.

CT scan.

CT scan with contrast.

MRI.

X-rays.

Blood work.

Poking.

Prodding.

What infection? Where? How to fight it?

As a tech wheeled me away for another test, Dad called Uncle Ronnie and gave him the update. He warned Uncle Ronnie to downplay everything when Mom called. No need in scaring Mom. Little existed for her to do from the road except worry.

True to her word, Mom called home when they stopped. Of course, she got no answer. So, she did exactly what Dad anticipated: she called Uncle Ronnie.

And Uncle Ronnie performed.

"Travis's eye didn't get any better," Uncle Ronnie said. "The doctor thought he oughta get checked out in Lexington, so Larry took him on over there."

All, technically, true.

Somewhat satisfied, but with her intuition pushing her into constant prayer for me, Mom continued toward Myrtle Beach.

I continued to submit to tests. The hours dragged on into nighttime. Dr. Browning came into the room and informed Dad I'd be admitted to the Pediatric ICU in order to isolate me and allow my body to fight the meningitis.

An orderly wheeled me down the hallway to the elevator.

"You should get them to take you up to the top of the hospital tower to see the fireworks from Red Mile," he advised. "Best place in the city to watch those."

If I thought hard enough, I could see the fireworks from last year in my mind's eye. Red, white, blue, gold, pink, and green bursts. Fourth of July, here again. We should be grilling in the garage. Burgers. Hot dogs. Baked beans. Mom's potato salad. Banana pudding. Putting the chairs in the car. Driving downtown for the fireworks. Writing our names in the air with sprinklers.

But I craved a cool darkness. A quiet place. An oasis. I closed my eyes against the light. It hurt to look.

Aunt Helen and Eddie left. Another MRI. Another CT scan. My fever spiked to 105.3. The white blood cells raged through my body, doing their best to stamp out the invader by any means—burn it up, explode it, whatever worked. I lay in a pool of misery, barely caring when a tube was inserted into my nose to give them a better view of the inferno roaring in my head. The medical experts, too, threw everything they had at the monster.

Antibiotics strong enough for a man twice my size.

Cooling blankets on my body.

A cooling mattress beneath me.

But my infection didn't blink. It raged and grew.

Nearly to Myrtle Beach, the church crew stopped once more. Mom dashed to a phone and called home.

Uncle Ronnie told her, "They've admitted Travis to the ER, Mary. He has some kind of infection. They don't know exactly what it is yet, but he's going to be okay."

Mom didn't quite buy Uncle Ronnie's latest performance. A picture of me lying in bed with a slightly swollen eye but a headache-free brain played through her memory. Clearly, the situation had deteriorated if now—after all those calls and all that effort she'd made—I'd become an admitted patient of the hospital in Lexington.

Mom called the Myrtle Beach airport and asked for the first flight home.

"The last flight out today left fifteen minutes ago," she heard. "The next flight is at 7 a.m."

Mom booked it and set her mind toward the promise she'd made me.

She needed to find something to bring back to her boy.

She joined a few of the youth at a souvenir shop and began the hunt. After selecting a pullover and green shorts, she made her way to the counter.

A young woman peered at Mom as she rang up her purchases. "Are you really a prayer warrior?" she asked.

Mom, head-deep in worry over me, didn't comprehend the question. "Excuse me?"

"Your shirt." The girl gestured to Mom's t-shirt. "Are you really a prayer warrior?"

Mom blinked. "Well, yes. Yes, I am."

The girl hesitated.

Mom eyed her piercings and colored hair, waiting.

"I need prayer," the girl blurted. "I haven't been a very good person."

Mom listened to the girl's life story of brokenness and pain birthed by poor choices and poorer circumstances. She silently asked God for wisdom. Why did He have her here, at this counter, when her boy lay crying in a hospital bed hundreds of miles away?

A whisper of an answer swept across her soul. She smiled a little smile. She couldn't hold my hand in that moment, but she *could* hold the one in front of her. Mom reached her hand across the counter and smiled. "Can I pray for you?"

Meanwhile, back in ICU, more specialists joined in the all-out race to identify my infection and find a treatment. Heat rolled off my body as my fever inched on up toward 106. The doctors worried about brain damage even *if* they got things under control at this point.

Dr. Wong, an infectious disease specialist, joined Dr. Wilson, a pediatrician, and Dr. Hayden, an ENT doc. They stared at my scans, talked, and stared some more. They stepped into my room, instructing Dad to step outside so they could shine a light into my eyes or stick another tube up my nose and freely discuss their ideas.

Dad took deep breaths. He prayed. He begged God to be with the doctors and nurses, to give them wisdom and understanding and a plan of action. To bring Mom home safely. To protect me. To protect her.

As he prayed, my eyes swelled shut. My eyelashes disappeared behind puffy skin.

The doctors left, telling Dad on their way out that he could come back in. Dad entered my frigid room, kept cold in a desperate yet vain attempt to get control of the fever. He skirted around the foot of my bed and sat down in the chair at my bedside. Taking my hand, he rested his head on the bed, took up his prayer again, and let the tears fall.

Pam, my main nurse, returned to check my vitals—not good—and noticed Dad freezing by my bedside. A mother of eight children, Pam knew a thing or two about raising kids and envisioned the nightmare Dad now found himself living.

She touched Dad's arm to get his attention.

He raised his head, startled.

"Could I get you a blanket?"

Dad nodded, then gazed toward me. My face no longer looked like Travis. This wasn't the boy who ran all over the neighborhood, who told stories about what he would do when finally he became a Corbin Redhound, who skied and laughed and played.

And lived.

"Dear God," he whispered, "let him live."

While Dad prayed on and Mom waited out the hours to board a plane, Dr. Hayden landed on a diagnosis: Cavernous Sinus Thrombosis.

An infection of the sphenoid sinus is a common occurrence usually cleared up within a few days by antibiotics. People get them all the time. CST, however, is quite rare. CST is blood clots in the veins or arteries in the Cavernous Sinus.

My initial infection had lain stealthily in my head for a week and a half, showing its face only in the form of a headache. By not revealing any of its telltale symptoms, it bought plenty of time to take up residence and morph into a dangerous sickness spawning blood clots.

Dr. Hayden didn't immediately relay this information to Dad. Only one person in the world, to that point, had battled CST of this magnitude and escaped with his mind intact. The high, prolonged fever typically left brain damage in its wake. A patient left behind in a vegetative state. More often than not—70% of the time—the patient died.

Of all five senses (sight, smell, touch, taste, hearing), only one sends its information directly into the brain: sight. This is done via a main nerve that lies at the base of the brain in front, right behind the eyes. An optic nerves goes directly from the eye, through the sphenoid sinus, and into the brain.

Which means that whatever a person allows himself to look upon goes directly into his brain. Unlike the other senses, there is no communication through the central nervous system, to the brain, and then back out to filter the information received through the sense.

See something, and boom, the brain sees it.

Or, in my case, catch something that's throwing blood clots into that artery and, boom, the brain gets it. One wrong clot and life terminates on this side of Heaven. Rather than bombard my body with antibiotics to treat bacterial meningitis that he now thought I didn't have, Dr. Hayden and the team kept up the antibiotics for one purpose: kill the CST before it killed me.

Mom called the hospital around midnight and managed to get Dad on the phone. Dad debated how much to tell her, torn between shielding the love of his life from the hell in my room and sincerely wanting his life partner to be fully present and in the battle with him.

He shielded her as best he could. "We're in the hospital and they're still running tests," he said. He told her of my high fever, of their suspicion of bacterial meningitis. And then he told her the one thing he absolutely knew.

"It's bad."

Dad stayed by my side through the night, stirring each time the doctors came in, propped open my swollen eyes, and shone a light into them. Seconds felt like minutes to him. Minutes felt like hours. He watched my monitors, sitting silently as time ticked on.

As Dad kept his lonely vigil, the world began dimming for me—blood clots forming on my retinas and cutting off the lifeblood to my optic nerves—but I didn't come out of my pain-induced stupor far enough to tell anyone.

Aunt Helen picked Mom up at the airport and had her at the hospital before 10 a.m. She'd been gone just one day. As she walked down the ICU hallway, Dad exited my room and saw her.

Knowing his ability to hide my condition from her had reached an end, he sobbed. "He's bad, Mary. He's swollen and he doesn't look like our Travis."

"What? What do you mean?" Mom looked from a broken Dad to my hospital door, anxious to get to me but a little fearful of what she'd find. "What's going on?"

"His fever is still really high. It has been all night. They're trying to cool him down, but he's not getting better. I just want to prepare you."

Mom swallowed hard. Hugged Dad harder.

Then she tiptoed into my frigid room.

I lay very still, long past any desire to move. Mere slits lay where my eyes had been. My cheeks puffed out as if I held air in them. Tubes sprouted all over my body, delivering help and whisking away invaders. A silver cooling blanket lay on me, but she could see my neck and head, and the paleness of my skin terrified her. Her eyes followed the tubes to blinking machines. The drastic change to my body in 24 hours slammed home the truth Dad had spoken: It's bad.

Mom arrived at my side and took my swollen hand in hers. She'd barely registered the nightmare when the bedside phone rang. She answered automatically, holding the phone between her and Dad, while Dr. Hayden informed them that he would be at the hospital soon.

They'd considered all the options and decided on the only one that offered even a possibility of hope: surgery. A team would gather as fast as possible.

He explained to Dad and Mom that he needed to go in and clean the infection out of the area behind my eyes and out of the sinuses. He hoped this would relieve the pressure and prevent clots from forming and going to my brain. The antibiotics weren't working. The cooling blankets weren't working. Nothing was working. Surgery offered a glimmer of chance to buy me some time.

My parents listened in a daze, nodding and signing the

necessary forms.

"It should take about an hour and a half," they were told. "We'll go in as soon as the surgical team gets here."

He meant as soon as they left their Fourth of July family barbecues. No time to waste on celebrations of independence. I didn't have the luxury of waiting until the fifth.

Around noon, an orderly came to get me. I managed to open my eyes enough to see Mom's face.

She was crying, but smiling at me.

"Don't worry, Mom. I'm going to be okay," I assured her.

"I love you, Travis," she said.

Her beautiful face would be the last image I ever saw.

As the surgeon placed a scalpel by my left eye and pressed down through my nose and into the top of my mouth, the surgical clock began ticking. Dad and Mom had retreated to the waiting room and joined the rest of the family. Time to wait out the hour and a half of my surgery. Aunt Helen, Eddie, their son Eddie Wayne, and Eddie Wayne's girlfriend all drove in. Uncle Durk and Aunt Sandra came.

They paced. They sat. They propped each other up. When the clock revealed two hours had passed, Eddie assured everyone that this could only be good. "It's good that it's taking so long," he said. Everyone wanted to believe him.

Hour three slipped by with still no word from the operating room. My family prayed on, begging God to spare my life. They were all blissfully ignorant of any possible outcome of surgery other than live or die. They only wanted me to live. It did not dawn on them I could be handed a very different kind of life.

At hour four, the tension in the waiting room could be cut with a knife. Eddie's assurances fell on deaf ears. What could be taking so long? Was it worse than they'd feared? How much worse? They paced some more. Prayed some more.

Finally, four and a half hours after I'd assured Mom I would be okay, Drs. Conklin and Hayden entered the waiting room and motioned my parents into the hallway.

"We took out as much of the infection as we could get," Dr. Hayden told them. "We don't know how much of his eyesight we saved, if any."

The world once again tilted for my parents. Saving my eyesight? What did that mean? Since when was there a battle for my eyesight? The battle was for my life, right?

The doctors explained more, but nothing else registered. They only wanted to get back to me, to touch me and assure themselves I'd made it through alive. They nodded through the words, waiting until they'd come to an end and the doctors walked away.

An hour after they'd learned I could be partially or completely blind—but alive—a nurse came to bring my parents to my bedside.

They stopped and stared at the pitiful form before them.

Packing stuffed my nose, and a big bandage swooped over my eye. More packing in my gums. A tube snaked from my nose, draining the remaining infection. None of the swelling had eased. Nurses bustled around me, checking dressings and monitoring vitals. My fever danced between 105 and 106, defying the antibiotics.

As a nurse leaned over me and shone a light into my eyes for the first of what would be hourly checks, Mom and Dad held on to the one glorious truth they could. The only truth that mattered. The oasis inside our swirling sandstorm.

He's alive.

5

LIGHTS OUT

COMMUNITY PULLS US THROUGH THE DRY STRETCHES. PIC-
ture a marathon runner, parched and tired, trying to dig deep
and find some energy for those last few miles. Then he sees a
hand on the side, offering a cup of water.

The runner snatches the water, never slowing, never falter-
ing. He gulps it. Pours the rest over his head. He is ready again.
He's renewed for the challenge ahead.

Because of community.

With the news I'd made it through surgery alive, most of the
family returned home except for Aunt Sandra and Uncle Durk.
They refused to leave in case things suddenly went south.

Mom and Dad called the church with an update on my condition and a request to pray. We needed my fever to break. The
threat of brain damage hovered over me each minute my body
stayed at 106 degrees. Brother Terry shared the news and asked
folks to come to the altar to lift me in prayer.

Bob and Karen Zik walked forward with the rest of the con-
gregation and knelt at the altar. When they stood, Karen leaned
in to Bob and whispered, "We have to go to the hospital tonight."

Bob stared at her. "Karen, we have five children," he reminded
her. Yet they both knew the fear my parents faced. Their twins
were triplets; one hadn't made it. Karen, a nurse, fervently wished
to be by Mom's side in case anything needed explaining or Mom
just wanted someone to lean on.

Within ten minutes of the final amen, all five Zik children scampered off to friends' homes to for the evening. The Ziks hit the interstate and headed north.

They arrived at about 10 p.m. that Sunday night. With someone now on hand for the night shift, Aunt Sandra and Uncle Durk retired to their car in the parking lot, where they would (unbeknownst to Mom and Dad) spend the night.

Pam, my main nurse, entered and told Mom and Dad to get some rest.

Dad had been awake since dropping Mom off in the church parking lot Saturday morning. Nothing made sense to him at this point. Up was down. Out was in. Night was day. He and Mom joined Bob and Karen in the waiting room and lay down.

Throughout the night, Karen answered Mom's questions about my condition and the activity of the nurses.

When you're caught between oases, head deep in a crack in the desert floor. It's good to have a friend who can explain the path ahead.

As the sun rose on Monday, July 6, Aunt Sandra and Uncle Durk climbed out of their car. They walked across the hospital parking lot and took the elevator back to the ICU waiting room. At their surprise appearance, Bob and Karen packed up their belongings. Karen hugged Mom and smiled, told her to call with any further questions, and they left.

While the changing of the guard occurred in the waiting room, a plane from New York landed in Lexington. On board rode a specialist steeped in knowledge about my condition. He drove to the hospital and examined me thoroughly, shining more light into my eyes and testing my optic nerves.

After much poking and prodding, he stepped away from my bed and left the room. He delivered his findings to Dr. Conklin, who then visited my room and asked my parents to join him in the hallway to discuss my condition.

They refused. "We do everything as a family," they informed the doctor. "Tell us here, where Travis can hear you, too."

There, standing over my bed, Dr. Conklin delivered the findings that he and the specialist had reached.

"Barring a miracle, Travis will never see again."

Chasing the gloom of my own pain, swimming in a sea of darkness, I didn't even hear him.

But Mom and Dad did. They listened as his words fell into the room. They weighed the sounds, unable to quite grasp their meaning in the immediate or long term. Not see at all? Ever?

Nothing more could be done.

As he left, my fever finally broke.

Living in a Sightless World

I woke up to darkness. All these years later, I like the spiritual bent to the sentence. I think it is one every person needs to utter at some point: Wake up to your darkness.

At twelve years old, with a heart devoted to the Lord and my ability to see forever gone, the darkness I woke to that Monday was literal.

Before I could truly grasp my new reality, Dad noticed I'd awakened. "Travis, do you remember what Dr. Conklin told us yesterday?"

"No," I responded. Hysteria crept at the edges of my consciousness. Why was everything so dark? I blinked. Blinked again. Nothing.

"He told us that, barring a miracle, you will never see again. The surgery saved your life, but the infection took your sight."

Comprehension dawned. My response crossed my lips with little thought.

"I believe I'll see again," I said. "But if I don't, I can't wait to see what God's going to do with my life."

Mom and Dad tucked my words away, into the same pocket as those of the doctor. *What did he mean? How did he come to say that?*

I don't have a recollection of saying that to Mom and Dad. I don't have a clear, uninterrupted recollection of the full three to four days after my initial surgery. I think, though, that my words had much to do with the reality of a year spent rising an hour early each morning, reading the Word, and talking with God. It did not dawn on me to doubt His presence or involvement in my life. It only occurred to me to wonder what He would do with what the world had dealt.

On Tuesday, after a mountain of ice chips and gallons of Jell-o were introduced to my system and welcomed in, I began to beg for the only thing I wanted: my catheter removed. I promised over and over I would ensure I performed bodily functions if they would just remove it.

I eventually won the prize. And then I got another one: removal from ICU. A regular room!

Dr. Blake dropped by to ensure I'd gotten settled into the new digs and ask how I was feeling. I told him a joke that involved Michael Jordan, Charles Barkley, and gambling. He responded in shock. How could I be trying to make him feel better? How could I be in good spirits?

I knew he felt horrible about the loss of my sight. He stood at the foot of my bed and cried. "Travis, I'm so sorry I couldn't do more."

"It's okay, Dr. Blake," I assured him. "I'm going to be fine."

The nurses brought recliners into my room so Mom and Dad could sleep in there with me instead of going to the waiting room to catch naps. With my life saved, we could focus on the next issue to overcome: the blindness.

Psychiatrists and psychologists came to see me. They spoke in hushed tones to Mom and Dad, warning them I would grow despondent, depressed, and angry. I might possibly even lash out. All part of the process, they said. To be expected.

Mom tried to match their words with the boy she knew and loved. "What if he doesn't?"

"Doesn't what?"

"What if he doesn't get angry and depressed and all these things you're saying?"

They peered at her as if she'd sprouted two more heads.

"He'd be the first," they said.

She sent them away. We'd take this one day—one hour—at a time.

I'd only been in ICU a couple of days when Dr. Conklin returned with an idea. He'd read of another CST case where someone lost his sight. Placement in a hyperbaric chamber for treatments on three consecutive days restored his vision. The highly pressurized oxygen atmosphere surrounding a patient in a hyperbaric chamber caused rapid healing and regeneration. Would I be willing to try it?

We initially agreed.

I *hated* it. Even writing about it makes me anxious. The chamber is entirely confining, like what I imagine a casket must feel like. I couldn't shake the notion that I'd get stuck or need something and no one would pull me out.

Dr. Conklin returned to my room and asked if I would do another treatment in the hyperbaric chamber.

At the same time, my parents and I replied. "No!"

Despite the warnings the psychologists gave to Mom, I did not grow depressed.

Mom read to me the stacks of cards that showed up from Corbin neighbors and family. She introduced me to audio books. With a grin, I chose *Jurassic Park* as my first one to hear. I encouraged Dr. Wong to watch the movie, remembering the incredible special effects stored away in my memory.

He went to see it, came to my room the next day, and told me it scared the—well, I won't say his exact words, but the movie terrified him.

My best friend, Josh Moran, called and asked to visit. I asked Mom to tell him not to come. I didn't want to see friends. I couldn't look at myself in the mirror, but I could touch my face and the puffiness there told me the Stay-Puft Marshmallow Man and I might share something in common. I also didn't know how to interact with my friends yet. How would it go? What would we talk about if I couldn't see? What would they think about all this? I didn't know what stirred inside me; I couldn't reassure them.

The pain and effort to heal required enough attention. I didn't feel ready to face the task of navigating friendships blind.

Then, early in the second week of regular room, Dad opened my hospital room door to find Jerry Allen Baker on the other side.

"Hi, Larry," Jerry said. "My aunt Linda dropped me off here. Thought I'd come see Travis."

Just like that, Jerry arrived. No questions. No plan. No checking to see if I wanted visitors. He decided I needed a friend and he came. He swiped a wheelchair from the hallway and helped me into it.

Then he wheeled me all around the hospital halls. His energy and zest for life reminded me I'd be out of there soon enough, back to fun and wringing every ounce of adventure from life that I could. As we zoomed up and down halls, Jerry described what we passed and made the visual world exist for me again. We didn't talk about what happened. He didn't ask me how I felt or what I'd been through.

Jerry just showed up and swept me back into life.

I will always love him for that.

Just because I'd made it through the life-saving surgery did not mean my medical journey had reached an end. Far from it. The same week of Jerry's visit, I underwent a second surgery to clean the infection from my sinuses again.

We spent the days shuttling back and forth across Limestone Street, from the hospital to Dr. Hayden's office and back. He tested my hearing, wondering if I'd also lose that sense.

Rather than losing my hearing, I sensed sounds more. I mined them for information. One of my usual orderlies loved comic book characters and could imitate their sounds amazingly well. He entertained me often. As the crazy orderly pushed my wheelchair from my room, through the viaduct across Limestone Street, and to Dr. Conklin's or Dr. Hayden's office, I could hear the differences in sound and tell when we moved from one area to the next. I learned to listen to the orderly's comedic imitations and laugh in response, even while keeping one ear tuned to the differences in my location.

Already, I'd begun to use another sense more strongly.

The Sunday after Jerry broke the "no visitors" barrier, a big group of my friends descended on my hospital room for a visit. They sat by me, and we talked as if nothing had happened. They were as normal and accepting to me as they could be.

Others made the long drive as well. Dad's boss, Paul Keller, came about every two to three days. Our family friend, Chad Woods, came nearly every day, armed with the food and snacks I liked. Poor Matt and Staci walked in with their parents, Sherry and David, on a day that the doctors had determined a need to draw blood from the artery (rather than vein) in my left wrist.

I'd been experiencing some pain in my shoulder that the doctors didn't understand. The last time I had pain without cause, it hadn't ended well. So, now, they took the hunt for the cause of any pain very, very seriously. My arms had holes in the bends from the twice-daily blood draws. This time, though, they were doing a blood gas to try to determine the cause of pain in my shoulder.

A blood gas measures the acid base in the blood. The problem is that blood must be drawn from an artery—rather than a vein—to run the test.

It HURT! It hurt so badly that I had no strength left to talk with Matt and Staci when they were finally allowed into the room.

One day I even got a phone call from UK's head coach at the time, Bill Curry. Dr. Conklin had told him about my ordeal, and he just wanted to call with some encouragement. He invited me to attend a game, and once I got better, I attended the UK vs. LSU game later that year. UK basketball legend Richie Farmer called to invite me to his basketball camp, but my hospital visit prevented my going.

People just kept coming, as did the balloons. Every day brought more balloons and more people. Each night, Dad and Mom sat by my bed and, together, we'd add to the list of what and who had visited.

Dad and Mom took turns feeding me. I had no idea how to do it without sight and made an awful mess when I tried. Gatorade and bags of mini Reese's Cups became my go-to fuel. Steroids zoomed through my IV, combating the swelling and making my appetite grow. I ate two breakfasts, two lunches, and two dinners each day and still kept losing weight.

Seventeen days after I'd entered the emergency room, the doctors discharged me from UK Medical Center with a slip of paper in my hand bearing contact information for a lady in Lexington. She'd teach me how to be blind and instruct my parents how to live with a blind person.

I'd entered the hospital full of sickness and disease. I left all of it behind—along with my sight—on a beautiful, sunny Tuesday.

At least Mom said it was a beautiful, sunny day. When we exited the hospital, I tilted my face up and felt the sun, instinctively "seeing" the world through a different sense.

"I want a cane," I said.

"A cane? What for?" Mom asked.

We hadn't yet spoken to experts and specialists about how to live as a blind person. The urge for a cane was just there, sitting in my brain, needing a voice.

"I'll need it to get around."

We drove to Grogan's and picked out a cane. I had no clue how to use it, but I had it, and I determined I could learn.

We hustled back into the car and ended up at McDonald's. A strawberry milkshake made me know I could still find some semblance of normal on the planet.

Now, to find out if I could create "normal" back in Corbin.

6

WALKING BY FAITH, NOT BY SIGHT

"Oh, Travis," Mom said.

At the sound of her voice, I rose from my place in the back seat.

"There's a sign hanging over the front door that says, 'Welcome home, Travis.'"

I smiled in spite of the pain and exhaustion. Home. After thirteen days in the hospital, we'd made it home. My bed would feel so good after all that time on a thin hospital mattress. No more hyperbaric chamber coffins. No more needles. I'd survived. All I needed to do now was learn to live.

Mom guided me out of the car and up the steps.

Dad opened the front door to an eerie silence. "There's another sign," Mom said softly. "It's hanging across the hallway—like the ones at the football games—and it says, 'Welcome home.'"

I stepped forward, out of Mom's grasp, and plowed through the paper barrier.

"Surprise!" yelled a rowdy chorus.

I jumped. So loud. So many. Here for me?

Mom led me to the loveseat and put my hand on its arm.

"Happy to have you home," Uncle Ronnie said.

"Happier to be here," I returned.

As our family, neighbors, and friends caught up with each other, I allowed myself to fall into the soothing comfort of home. I'd missed them more than I realized. Though they'd visited the hospital faithfully, their voices didn't sound the same bouncing off tile floors and sterile walls through the smell of antiseptic. Here, they reassumed their usual richness of texture and ease.

"I'm going to my room," I announced after an hour, and I stood up. Immediately, friends took my arms. That annoyed me. I shrugged them off.

"I don't need your help getting through my own house," I snapped.

The room descended into silence. I sighed and shook my head. The therapists told Mom I'd be mad about the blindness. I hadn't yet felt that, but my frustration with people assuming my mind disappeared with my sight grew each day.

"I'm sorry," I said as I felt my way out of the room and down the hallway, picking up speed with each successful step. "I just don't need the help. Thanks."

I plunged into my bedroom.

Smack into toilet paper strung everywhere.

This time, I recognized the eerie silence. "You guys!"

The beautiful sound of my friends' laughter burst all around me. They'd snuck in while I made my way into the room.

"We couldn't resist!"

"We're sorry if this was mean!"

I shook my head. "It's not mean. Y'all are just nuts."

And you'd pull this kind of stunt on anybody, so I love it.

I laughed, untangled myself, and sprawled across the bed.

"We'll let you get some rest."

"Thanks."

I listened to them shuffle out the door. Good people. Good friends. Relationships. Help for the arid path ahead.

For the next two weeks, the doorbell rang constantly. Each time Mom opened the door, another friend stood on the doorstep, meal in hand. Our refrigerator filled up. Our freezer filled up. The extra refrigerator and freezer in the garage filled up. And still they came. "How's Travis? How are you? What can we do?"

Hands holding out cups of water for us to finish our race.

While Mom socked away food and told our story over and over, I turned my focus toward the looming challenge coming down the pike.

Seventh grade.

Without football.

"Want to go for a drive?" Dad asked one day. I hadn't been out of the house much. A drive didn't require that I navigate the world, just sit and listen.

"Sure."

We all hustled out to the car. With the windows down, I lifted my face toward the breeze and breathed in deeply. It smelled like home. Rich dirt, clean water, and lush trees. I heard the rattling mufflers of old trucks on the road. The talking and laughing as our little town went about its day.

I smiled. Corbin. I needed to remember the town and my love for it.

Dad drove around downtown, with Mom narrating as we went.

"There's the grocery store."

"We're passing by the Pepsi plant."

I could see it all in the darkness of my mind, pictures coming to life with her words.

Her narration ceased. And then I heard its cause.

The sharp shrill of a whistle blow. "Gimme four laps!" The clatter of pads and equipment on the move.

"Is the team out there?" I asked, hearing them.

"Yes," Mom replied. "They're practicing."

I grew quiet, pulling back into the car. Clearly, my dream of being a Corbin Redhound stayed behind at the hospital, cut away and left on the operating room floor. I tried to envision seventh grade without sports. Nothing about the notion felt right. But how could I be a Redhound now? How could I even walk around the school? Maybe they'd let me be a water boy. I remained quiet the rest of the drive – a silence that spoke volumes to my parents.

We returned home, and Mom helped me to the couch inside while Dad headed back to work. I fell asleep with visions of sitting on a bench, holding a water bottle out, and waiting for someone to take it from me.

Checking the paper she'd been given at the hospital, Mom left me sleeping and crept into her bedroom to call the blindness expert in Lexington.

"The first thing you need to do," the expert advised, "is realize you no longer have a son. Send him to the Kentucky School for the Blind where he'll learn to live in a dark, dark world. You are no longer a part of his life. The quicker you learn this, the better off you'll be."

Mom gasped. Give up her son? Not a chance in Hades. She and Dad hadn't stormed the gates of heaven – along with our church family – to beg for my life only to ship me off to some school where they'd never see me. Surely another solution existed.

As the expert rattled on about this new order of things and helpless tears streamed down Mom's cheeks, she switched to instinct mode.

Mom hung up.

Then she called Dad, sobbing with hiccupping gasps.

"Mary? What is it? Has something happened with Travis?"

Mom calmed down enough to explain her anguish. Apparently, they'd need to give me up. Take me to a school and leave me behind.

"Hold on," Dad said. "I'm coming home, and we'll have a family meeting."

Twenty minutes later, Dad joined Mom on their bedroom floor. They held each other and wept, trying hard to face the idea of separating from me. When their tears eased, they woke me for a family meeting. Dad told me about the call with the blindness expert in Lexington.

I burst into tears. "But I don't want to leave home!"

We all hated the idea, but the woman was an *expert* on how to navigate the rough patch of desert in which we found ourselves. She knew how to get through. We needed to pay attention and consider her words.

Mom called the Kentucky School for the Blind and arranged a visit.

The Kentucky School for the Blind is a wonderful place for the appropriate student. The three of us spent an entire day with them, touring the facility and asking questions. We came with the expectation of finding a prison-like structure. After all, why pay attention to aesthetics when the students can't see it to appreciate it?

Mom and Dad quickly let me know we'd underestimated KSB. Begun by Bryce Patten in 1839 and later established by the state legislature as the third school for the blind in the United States, KSB had moved to Frankfort Avenue in Louisville in 1855. The main white building rose five floors and bore a rotunda on top with a widow's perch. Its massive four white columns across the front greeted us with the reminder that, while we may be on an

5 weeks old in my UK hat

4 years old

4 years old

4 years old, ring bearer in a wedding

Camp Bethel, one month before I lost my eyesight

Greenwave 6th grade football

5th grade football Greenwave

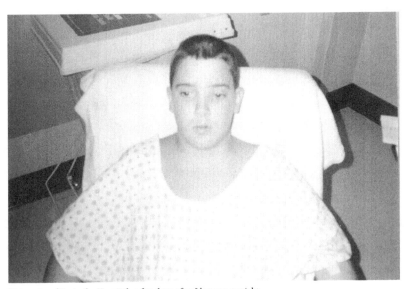

University of Kentucky Hospital, a few days after I lost my eyesight

Nurses at the UK Hospital

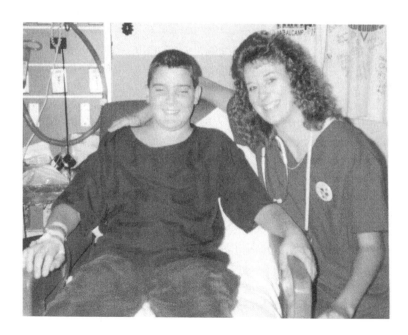

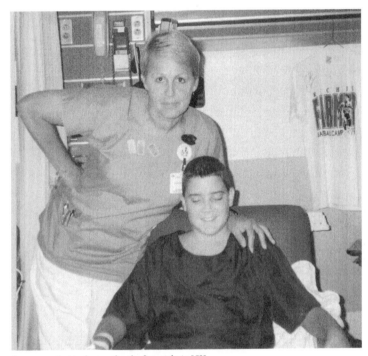

Pam, nurse that took care of us the first night in ICU

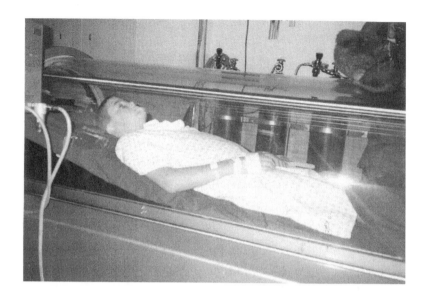

Hyperbaric oxygen chamber

Lexington Mall, Josh Moran, Jerry Baker, Chad Faulkner, Larry and me

Lexington Mall, Larry and me

Jerry Baker and me (I'm guiding)

1998 Corbin High School Varsity Football Team

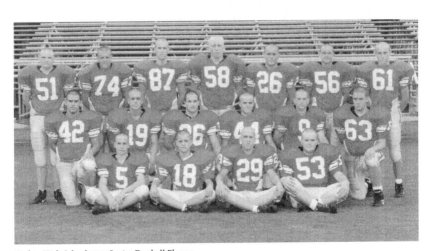

Corbin High School 1998 Senior Football Players

Larry and me, Texas Stadium, Dallas Cowboys game 1996

Senior Football Picture

Me with two of my best friends, Derrick Neal and Josh Moran

Senior year 1998-1999

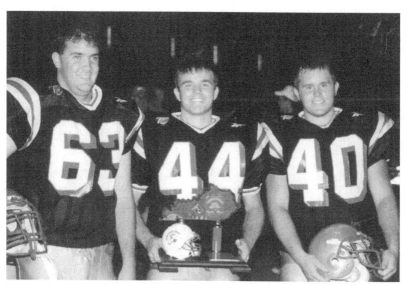

Me, Derrick Neal and Mike Neal

Me with Staci Logan

Washington DC at the Vietnam Memorial Wall, 1999

1998 Prom

Josh Moran, Derrick Neal, me, and Rob Taylor, 1998 Prom

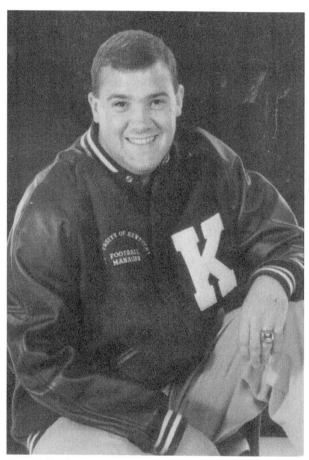

UK Football equipment manager, 1999-2003

Big Dipper All Mountain Team, 1998: Graham Trimble, Big Dipper, me, and Zac Prewitt

Nashville, TN, Music City Bowl, 1999

Ph.D graduation at The Southern Baptist Theological Seminary, May 2012

Master graduation at The Southern Baptist Theological Seminary, May 2007

Seminary President's Reception, May 2012: Mary, me, and Larry

Game photo, October 1998

Hiking trip, 2012, me, Durk Hopkins, Kelly Helton, Scott Clouse

On this trip Kelly and Scott had never been anywhere with me. They were amazed with my hiking skills, so they closed their eyes to see what I was experiencing. They fell and stumbled over everything. Hilarious according to Durk.

educational campus, we hadn't left the South.

I listened to Dad's and Mom's descriptions as we walked the wide pathways beneath enormous trees. I heard the birds singing and felt the sun on my face. Dad, while admitting to the beauty of the environment, never wavered from his core conviction: he hated the place and wanted nothing to do with it. Thankfully, the director of the school noticed early in our tour that I didn't quite fit the mold of a typical KSB student. While I had battled with 106 degree fever for days, I had escaped lasting brain damage. Nothing on me walked away from the ordeal damaged outside of the loss of my sight. Additionally, I'd enjoyed a healthy and full twelve years of life prior to losing my sight.

The director turned to my parents toward the end of our tour. "Look, Travis just doesn't belong here."

We breathed a collective sigh of relief.

"But what do we do?" Mom asked. "School starts soon. How will he get around the school? Take classes? Learn?"

We listened closely as the director shared the truth that, in Kentucky, the public school is required to provide what blind schoolchildren need to obtain an education (and is given money by the state to do so). The Corbin school system had to provide this training, though it would likely work with KSB to obtain such.

I had three weeks before school started. Seventh grade. I set aside football and turned my focus toward learning how to walk, eat, dress, shower, and navigate the world on my own again.

Meanwhile, word in Corbin had traveled. Travis is home. Travis is alive. Travis is blind. It seemed everyone knew...including the officials at school.

John Jones, handicap coordinator for Corbin and an assistant football coach, called a meeting with us and Principal Darrell

Termaine. Coach Jones proceeded to inform everyone that he'd arranged for a bus to pick me up on Sunday afternoons, take me to the Kentucky School for the Blind, and return me on Friday afternoon. My parents shook their heads.

"I don't think you understand," Mom said. "Travis will be going to school right here in Corbin, as he always has."

The principal smiled and jumped on board, moving the discussion into the details of how we would accomplish this plan. What classes would I have? Where would they be? Would someone need to take me? Would someone sit in class with me? How would I take notes? Find my locker? Navigate the hallways? The more the questions arose, the more overwhelmed Coach Jones felt.

Me, too, but no other choice existed. I didn't belong at KSB. I belonged in Corbin.

Mom and Dad accepted the best truth of my future and transmitted it to me: I would live sightless in a sighted world. They would let me go into it. We'd all have to learn how.

The first day of seventh grade came too quickly and not fast enough. I didn't feel ready. Would I ever feel ready, though? Probably not. Mom drove me to school and, just as I'd asked, she stayed. Also as I'd asked, she stayed *in the office.* Because, come on, what seventh-grade boy wants his mom hanging around— even if he's scared out of his mind and desperately, secretly *wants* her by his side?

We had two teams of teachers in the seventh grade. One team had two teachers, and the other had four. The principal thought it would be best for me to be on the team with two teachers. That way I would only have to go between two classes. But the team with four teachers wanted me. They went to the principal and asked him if he would put me on their team. He liked the fact that they wanted the challenge of teaching me, so I was placed on the team with Brenda Thomas, Cindy Creech, Sharon Ball, and Darlene McBurney. They accepted the challenge of being the first teachers in the Corbin City School System to teach a blind student.

Friends like Jerry Baker, Josh Moran, Zac Prewitt, Chad Faulkner, Ryan Ball, and Derrick Neal and teachers helped me get from class to class the first few days. I probably had fifteen new bruises by the end of the week. Clearly, I needed some help in how to walk with the cane and get from place to place.

Enter Patty Wheatley. Patty's husband was one of nine children, five of whom were blind. She would serve as my Orientation and Mobility Instructor. Within a couple weeks of starting school, Patty began coming to Corbin to give me back independent mobility.

She taught me how to use the cane, that every time I take a step the cane sweeps the floor. It is like you are kicking the cane back and forth between your feet. She also made sure that my cane was the right height (mid-chest) for me. She taught me how to "feel" driveways along the street and thus judge where I'd walked, and she taught me to put a hand in front of my face when I bent over to pick up something on the floor so I wouldn't hit my head on anything on the way down.

"Always feel a seat before sitting," she'd say, "to make sure it's empty. Place a finger over the edge of a glass you're filling so that you'll know when it is full."

She advised me to look at a plate of food like a clock. People could tell me where food is in reference to time. (This is assuming the person can tell time, of course. I've found some that have trouble with this.)

She put me in situations that I would have to figure a way out of. I had to learn to think critically to escape or handle the situation. One day, she gave me a bill to pay and money to deposit at the bank. She did not tell me where to go. I knew how to get to the bank, and so I walked there first. Then I asked the people at the bank how to get to the Kentucky Utilities Office. The people at the bank told me its location in reference to ours. I then had to follow their directions on my own and find the KU office. Patty followed along behind, silently watching, always ready to jump in if I wandered into danger.

She also taught me proper sighted guide technique. That I should hold on to a person's arm when I walk with them. That when we are in narrow spaces, the person should put that arm behind their back so that I would get behind them. Also, when we get to a step, the guide stops for a split second in order to let me know the step is coming; then they stop again at the top or bottom of the steps so I know when they are over. If only the whole world knew these things!

One day not long into my instruction, Patty told me to walk to Matt and Stacie's, then walk to my grandmother's. These were houses I'd been to a million times when I could see. I'd lain on my grandmother's couch when the headache struck. Surely I could find my way there now.

I set off, swinging the cane with each step, feeling the texture of the ground in front of me and to the side. One driveway. Two. Three. I counted and turned corners, building a map in my mind of what I'd been able to see only a few weeks before. Here, in my mind, I could still see the world. I simply needed to marry the mental image to my present reality.

I walked and swung. Walked and counted. Walked and swung. Finally, I turned into a driveway.

"Yes!" Patty shouted from behind.

I'd made it to my grandmother's!

I might as well have been handed a football trophy. This world was different, but it didn't present an impossible challenge. Just a challenge I hadn't seen before.

Patty had imparted the most important lesson of all: I could be independent because there *is* a way to make *anything* happen.

Three weeks into the new school year, I felt safe and prepared enough to go solo. Mom went back to work. I eased into my new life, hanging out with friends again and adjusting to the new methods of learning and moving. My parents allowed friends to come visit, and life—an altered life—began to hum along again.

Patty and I continued to work together on through the winter with her visiting Corbin once a week. In February, she declared she'd taught me all she could in Corbin and required me to travel to Lexington for our last three lessons: Riding Public Transit, Getting Around a Mall, and Riding a Greyhound Bus.

Josh Moran, Jerry Baker, and Chad Faulkner went with us to the mall. Patty greeted us with blindfolds in hand and cheerfully declared, "Okay, y'all, welcome to Travis' world."

She paired us off, then blindfolded one person in each pair.

"Now y'all who can still see will lead the ones whose sight has been taken. We'll flip the other way in a little while. Everybody ready? Your first task is to find the food court."

Off we headed—right into benches and people and signs and strollers and anything else that happened to be in our path. My friends fell all over everything, including into a garbage can.

My laughter roared down the concourse. *Not so easy, is it, guys?*

I suddenly didn't feel quite so alone—or odd for taking a while to adjust to life without sight. While they could never completely grasp my condition (they could, after all, take off the blindfold if something difficult arose), they had a taste of it now. That taste put them at my table for the briefest of whiles. It felt good to be in company.

Patty insisted that I learn Braille.

I objected.

She insisted.

I griped to Mom, who went to Patty, who insisted.

For the record, I don't care for Braille. It's tedious and time-consuming. It is impossible to rush through. It requires focus to the exclusion of others to gain understanding. However, a blind person is classified as illiterate unless he/she can read Braille.

Illiterate!

So, with an enormous sigh, I put my fingers to the task. I learned Braille.

And in my later years I have learned to appreciate it more. I wish I could be faster at reading it. It could help me a lot in my preaching at times. But I don't wish that hard enough to spend more time with it.

As I began to walk with more confidence and grew in the knowledge that a dark world isn't an impossible one, I began to learn just how blind everyone around me acted.

The police station received phone calls. "That blind kid is walking on Kentucky Avenue," a kind citizen reported. "He's gonna get killed."

No, actually, I'm not. I didn't lose my mental faculties or my ability to walk. I can still hear traffic and use all my senses to determine where I am and whether I'm safe.

I walked down a sidewalk and cars honked their horns at me. Yeah, I can hear your tires. No need for horns, thanks. Just like horns startle those who can see the car but don't expect a horn sound, they startle ones who can hear the car (thus see it in their mind) but also don't expect a horn sound.

I voiced my frustrations to Patty, who answered by teaching me along two tracks: how to see with my other senses, and how to handle the sighted world's "helps" along the way.

Those "helps" are my ongoing source of frustration.

Oddly, I didn't battle with anger at my condition. It's something I am often asked. "Do you ever wonder why it had to happen to you?" Well, no. "Do you ever get mad that this happened?" Well, no. What would be the point?

But I *do* get frustrated when people assume I can't do something just because I'm blind. People who have known me for years suddenly assume I'm a moron who can't open a jar of pickles. Close your eyes. Pick up a jar of pickles. Can you still open it? Me, too.

I don't want to give the wrong impression. Relearning how to walk, talk, dress myself, go to the bathroom, and just live presented serious challenges. Really hard. Definitely not all sunshine and roses. And some people were less ignorant of my condition and more downright mean.

A few weeks into school, a kid thought it would be funny to kick my cane out from under me.

He found it less hilarious when he found himself almost instantly thrown up against a locker and held there by Zac Prewitt, who growled, "Don't you ever touch him again."

The kid never did.

So, yeah, some moments felt darker than others. All in all, though, as the days of seventh grade reached their end, I slowly realized I'd adjusted. I still had my relationships with God, family, and friends. I'd grown very close to my Uncle Ronnie, who was wheelchair bound. We understood living life outside the realm of "normal."

Life rolled on.

Except for that one thing I missed more than ever: playing football.

We still attended the games. Dad described to me the action on the field as he and Mom watched. I cheered. I armchair quarterbacked. My dream of playing tickled my memory and I pushed away the loss. No sense in dwelling on it. *Let it go. Just let it go. Be grateful you are alive.*

But the longing remained. I wanted – needed – to be on that field.

I thought back to my first day home from the hospital. To the idea of helping the team in some way. Maybe go back to my days as a water boy. Anything to get me down there, with the team. At least *near* the Redhounds.

The seventh grade talent show came along, and I entered. I'd grown pretty adept with clay and could mold a Corbin Redhound out of model magic as fast as someone else fixed a cup of coffee. Maybe if I couldn't *be* a Redhound, I could create them with my own hands.

It didn't feel the same. It didn't quench the thirst. But it provided respite for a bit.

Mom watched my display of artistry (which would be awarded second place), and inwardly ached that I could no longer be a Redhound on the field. Mom spotted Coach Farris and walked over to him. "Coach," she asked, "would it be possible for Travis to help out with the team somehow?" She gestured back at the stage, where I held up my new masterpiece. "He loves the team. Maybe he could manage the equipment or water or something?"

Coach Farris didn't hesitate. "No," he responded.

Before Mom could object, Coach continued, "But he can play."

He can *play.*

Hello, jersey #67!

7

CHASING LIFE IN THE DARK

THIS IS THE PART WHERE EYEBROWS ARE RAISED AND HEADS are scratched.

How does a boy who is blind play football?

Very carefully.

Just kidding—mostly.

There's no use pretending football is easy, even for the sighted. It's a hard game where the players spend most of their time being slammed to the ground or ramming their bodies against contraptions, getting better at throwing themselves into live human beings on the field.

It can be brutal. It can be dangerous.

So how does a boy who can't see insert himself into the mix of clashing helmets and colliding players? There is one position that doesn't require much use of sight. Just one. And Coach Farris had already thought about it.

"He'll play center," Coach told Mom. "I'll teach him."

I flew on the high of that offer right into my local pediatrician's office to obtain the required medical clearance for play.

Except he would have nothing to do with it.

"You're crazy," he told Mom. "He simply can't do this."

I crashed from the high of envisioning my return to the team, dissolving into tears in the back seat.

"Hang in there, Travis," Mom said. "He's not the only doctor."

She has a way of getting to the right person for the job, my mom. She called Dr. Hayden. "That's a wonderful idea!" Dr. Hayden responded. "Any player can—and does—get blindsided," Dr. Hayden said. "I'm happy to sign off on it. Good for Travis, and good for Coach Farris."

I soared back into the belief that very, very soon I'd be back on that field.

The first day of practice rolled around nearly three months later. A hot, humid early August day full of golden rays and promise. Cicadas buzzing in the bushes. Air thick with moisture that left me feeling like I'd had a shower just by walking to the mailbox.

I woke up with a lot of hope. There probably should have been a healthy dose of fear mixed in, but a thirteen-year-old doesn't fear much of anything. Besides, I'd already lived through the loss of my sight and very nearly my life. Danger on the gridiron paled in comparison.

Mom dropped me off at the little league baseball field where the team practiced. I navigated toward the sound of voices and received the reward of a greeting from Coach Farris. "Travis! Good to have you. Get to stretching."

That was it. No fanfare. No big speeches or announcements that the blind kid had arrived. No long ordeal and discussion about how this would work or who would help me out. Just another boy on the team.

Thank the Lord.

We stretched, then went into agility exercises like high steps and bear crawls. I already knew the routine, having completed it a million times my sixth-grade year. The motions returned to me easily, dredged up from my memory and moving my muscles automatically into rhythm. I listened carefully to the teammates around me. Heard them get winded, just like me. Heard Coach Farris' whistle and command to start a different exercise.

I'd not realized in my sighted years that so much of football requires listening more than seeing. In the few instances where a new exercise was instructed, I asked a teammate beside me to describe what to do. Coach never stopped practice to treat me any differently from the other players. He expected me to figure out a way to get the command done, just like everybody else. I didn't have to ask the guy next to me to describe something new before it became automatic for them. That's an incredibly cool thing about being on a team—you look out for each other. If they missed hearing a command, I told them what they'd missed. If I needed to know something that could only be seen, they informed me.

Coach Farris called one last exercise before ending our first practice. Sprints. I didn't know if I'd make it. A year on the sidelines had left me very out of shape. The guys around me huffed—I could hear it—but not like me. I was struggling, and I knew it.

But no scenario or requirement existed to get me off that field. I'd dreamt of being back, and I refused to walk off now or ask for special treatment. Not that Coach Farris would have given it, anyway.

I made it through sprint after sprint with barely time to marvel at one's completion before the next came. Finally, Coach blew the whistle for the last one.

Except I had no juice left. I'd already put everything onto the field. Everything. Not an ounce of ability remained in my body. I made it forward a few steps, then fell.

I got up, determined. I ran a few more feet.

And fell again.

I could balance. I knew where I was.

I simply had run out of energy.

I got up again.

Ran farther.

Fell again.

Up again.

Three steps.

Fell again.

Up again.

Five steps.

Fell again.

Up again.

Two steps.

Fell again.

Up again.

And again.

And again.

Turn around to run back.

Fall.

And get up.

And fall.

And get up.

With a final huff, I finished the last sprint and collapsed into the huddle.

"Freeman!" Coach barked. "Get up! You don't fall down in my huddle!"

No, Sir. Not me or any other player. I struggled to my feet, feeling the supportive arm of a teammate and knowing that, had the roles been reversed, I'd have done the same.

Teamwork. Community. Getting me through a desert stretch.

Coach released us. My teammate handed me off to Dad, who helped me into our gray Ford truck. I leaned against the door the entire way, eyes closed. He got me home and guided me into the door, where I collapsed onto the dining room floor.

I didn't move for half an hour. Then, restored by some time on the floor, I hit the shower.

In the beginning, I was kept away from the blocking sleds and instead sent to work with the quarterbacks and learn how to play center. Time to learn how to snap the ball.

Sounds pretty simple, right? Grab the ball. Snap it. Easy as pie. Until I tried it out for the first time.

The quarterback lined up behind me. I reached out, feeling for the ball—and instantly realized there are a *lot* of ways to mess this up.

If, in reaching out to find the ball, I inadvertently spin it or don't keep it parallel to the sidelines, it's a 5-yard penalty. If I lift or move the ball in any way other than to snap it and start the play, it's a 5-yard penalty. Try finding a football somewhere on the ground in front of you without lifting or moving it. I got very good at inching my feet side to side, forward, or backward to position my body in relation to the ball rather than the ball to my body. Once that ball is on the ground, it stays put until I snap it.

Then, of course, I have to snap it. It has to land safely in the hands of the quarterback so that he can execute the first step in the play. If you watch football, you'll see that sometimes Centers look back through their legs to gauge where the quarterback is. Of course, I didn't have that luxury. I needed to know where the quarterback would be for each play and he needed to be exactly where he should be.

For plays where the quarterback was positioned right behind me, I could push off his hands and ram into the guy in front of me. These were the easiest plays. The quarterback's hands were on my rear (as is true with any Center and Quarterback), so I knew exactly where to put the ball and precisely where to plow forward to make the tackle. Centers can attest, your hand naturally curves a bit when you snap the ball between your legs and behind you. It lands perfectly situated in the quarterback's hands for a pass or hand-off.

There are plays, though, where the quarterback positions himself a few yards behind the center. This requires a gun snap. The only way to accurately get the ball from the ground, between the center's legs, into the air, and safely into the hands of the quarterback is to practice.

We discussed it for a while. Was there any way that I could learn to do this? In the end, we had to admit that gun snaps require sight. We determined that shotgun plays would need to be handled by one of the other centers. Which meant we'd have to keep it to ourselves that I played blind. The other teams couldn't know.

With a very few weeks of practice under our belts, we prepared for the first game. I put on the #67 jersey, butterflies in my stomach like every other player. Our first game as eighth graders. In just a little while, we'd know if our practice had been good enough or not quite. We'd test our skills against a rival team. Were we ready?

Only one way to find out.

As the floodlights drew mosquitoes and hundreds of parents, friends, and family members filled the bleachers, our entry music blared through the speakers.

"Whoomp! There it is!" Tag Team sang as the announcer declared, "And here are your Corbin Redhounds!"

We dashed onto the field as one, ready to take on the battle before us.

We were a couple minutes into the second half when I heard Coach say, "Travis, you're in."

I slapped on my helmet and ran toward the sound of my teammates. Josh Moran grabbed my jersey and pulled me into the huddle. The quarterback told us the play. We broke, heading into the line.

I knew I could do this.

The guards on either side of me grabbed my jersey and pushed and pulled me into position. After hundreds of practice runs, I'd developed a natural instinct now to bend, touch the ball, shuffle my feet to be in better position, snap, and plow forward into the opposing player.

The lack of visual input allowed for me to go deeply inward, hearing the crash of helmets and huffs of out-of-breath players. I crystallized my thoughts and focus before snapping the ball as I'd been unable to do when my eyes worked.

We fought hard, crushing the other team and walking away victorious. Despite the positioning help from the guards, the other team never had a clue they faced a blind player.

I left the field feeling as if more than one battle had been won that night.

The season continued and, with the exception of two games, I saw field time in the second half of every one of them. Each time the buzzer blew, our team came away with a win, finishing the season undefeated. We celebrated on the field, then scurried home to furiously finish homework before school the next morning.

In the beginning of the season, a couple of parents worried for my safety and that of their sons. Actually, it was probably more than a couple but only that many voiced their concerns. How could this be? A blind center? Wouldn't he get hurt? What were his parents thinking?

My parents overheard the discussions at the field. Some parents even came to mine directly and questioned their sanity. But no one would have let it go on if it appeared that students were in danger.

Other than the danger of throwing their bodies at each other on purpose with every play, of course.

It only took a few games for them to see that things were working out. Yeah, I relied on the guards to get me to the huddle and position me on the line, but that's what teams do: help each other.

Only once did safety become an issue. Coach Farris wasn't at the game for some reason, so the assistant coach stepped up to handle the game against Pulaski County. One of their players kept grabbing the back of my helmet and throwing me to the ground. Our coach alerted the ref both to what was happening on the field and to the fact that I was blind. The ref pulled the entire opposing team to the side. "If I see another one of you touch his helmet," he warned them, "I'll throw every single one of you out of this game."

Internally, from the coaching staff to the team, no one ever questioned if I should or could play Center. Coach Farris brought me in and that was that.

I've thought about that since. With a different coach, I might not have been allowed near the team at all. Even if Mom had insisted I be allowed to hold water bottles, the coach calls the shots about the team. A good coach knows what will work for his team and what won't. He holds true to his gut and his own experiences.

Coach Farris did this. He saw a boy who needed to be a Corbin Redhound. Who had spent childhood in the stands and only had a taste of it in sixth grade.

He believed a way existed.

And because he believed, the way became clear.

We finished our football year by winning the conference championship.

Not a bad way to return to the game.

Not bad at all.

In addition to the challenges of football, the rest of life continued to bring its own set of obstacles to overcome. For instance: snow.

Our town was created for snow. Mountains rise up all around, creating perfect inclines for sledding. When the white stuff falls, we break out the big round disks and inner tubes and fly away.

Which is all well and good until you have no ability to see what you're flying *toward*.

The second winter after I lost my sight, we decided I could sled like everybody else. As soon as the right snowfall came, Matt, Staci, and I grabbed inner tubes and plodded over to a hilly section of the road in our neighborhood.

By "hilly", I mean an extremely steep incline that cars have trouble getting up when there *isn't* ice on the surface. Perfect spot to fly along packed ice crystals, right?

We thought so, too, and hopped on. For hours, we flew down, coasted to a stop, then trudged back up the hill to do it all over again. We wore down a rut of packed ice and snow that got slicker and faster as the minutes ticked away. Our parents came out, telling us to take our one last ride and call it a day. Matt went. Then Stacie.

And then it was my turn.

I hopped on my tube, the same as I'd been doing all day, and took off.

Except this time a car began backing out of a driveway at the end of the hill. A car I couldn't hear or see.

Which meant it was a car I would not attempt to avoid.

The car kept backing up, further and further into my path. I careened down the hill as Dad started screaming. "No! Stop! Stop!" He took off running, slipping and sliding in the snow, trying to get to me before impact.

But I was hurtling. Oblivious.

I slammed directly into the side of the car's back tire. My inner tube bounced off, tossing me into the air. My head hit the tire. I rolled and came to a stop.

Dazed, I lay still.

The woman driving the car opened her door and saw me lying still on the road. "Somebody call 911!" she screamed. "He's dead!"

I'm dead? This is death? That's it? No heaven?

I started screaming too.

Dad arrived seconds after impact. "He's not dead."

I calmed down. *Whew.*

I'd avoided death again. This time with another cut to my head.

Mom bore the brunt of most of the work required to keep me going. Moms do a lot of that. Being a sports parent comes with its own additional set of chores that millions of sports parents can attest to. Keep uniforms clean. Wash practice clothes. Have the right food and drinks on hand to replenish the body after practice or prepare it before a game. Get together all the support paraphernalia—player pins, sweatshirts, t-shirts, bleacher seats, etc. Keep track of the play schedule. Get us where we need to be on time and with the right equipment in our bags.

Lots of parents can push some of these responsibilities onto their child. But mine couldn't say, "Go look for your cleats and make sure to put them in your bag." If the cleats weren't where I remembered putting them, I couldn't look around and find them. I had to ask for help, and that help usually came from Mom.

Also, while I'd learned again how to eat and drink, I didn't do too well yet with making my own meals. Even putting a sandwich together wasn't worth the effort to find the right foods in the refrigerator, find the bread, find a plate, somehow assemble it all, and get everything back where it belonged. By the time I got all that done, the sun would have moved enough in the sky to warrant breakfast.

Mom soldiered on. This was our life now, and she would not be deterred from having life, and having it abundantly (as the Scriptures say). She didn't complain, at least as far as I know. She simply buckled down and kept doing the needed thing in front of her – even the extra things created by having a sightless son. Learning to put chairs back under the table when she got up so I didn't trip over them. Not leaving the vacuum cleaner out for me to fall over. Keeping everything in the same place in the house. Organizing cabinets and closets so that I could find towels and shoes. Making sure the knives were pointed down in the dishwasher in case, when she was unloading it, I tripped over it. Matching my clothes and keeping them together in the closet and drawers.

In addition to the new behaviors, numerous worries plagued her that went beyond those of parents of "normal" kids. I could get lost so easily. And if I did, how could I find someone to ask for help? How hurt would I be if she allowed me to attempt the latest crazy idea that popped into my head? Other parents let their kids try—but their kids could see danger if it popped up.

The crazy schedule and added demands began to take their toll. Working at the bank, volunteering at church, and being an involved wife and overly needed mother created a situation that fast approached insurmountable. Should Mom quit her job?

She and Dad began to discuss the possibility in fits and spurts. By the spring, they were talking about it openly with me as well. We all saw the wisdom in Mom coming home. But could we financially do it?

Life had surprised us by settling into happiness again. Despite my challenges and Mom's exhaustion, we had found our way into a fairly good spot. And if Mom was coming home, things would only get better.

Had the school year ended on that stellar note, I could end this chapter with a happy flourish.

But Dad came home one May day with crushing news.

"The company's been sold," he informed Mom and me. "My job is gone. My last day is September 30."

He'd been at Interstate Coal Company for eighteen years, rising to become Manager of Fixed Asset Accounting. None of us, including Dad, saw this coming. Why now? Right when things were finally beginning to enter some sense of normalcy again? I was getting around, having a life, being a Corbin Redhound. But without Dad's income, the future held only uncertainty.

Except God.

He hadn't left. He wasn't surprised. He had a plan.

Dad began looking for another job as we rolled into summer. I signed up for high school football and dreaded the start of Two-A-Days that were coming in eight weeks.

Two-A-Days are sometimes called Hell Week. They're about as close as a player can get to walking in that fiery place without actually going there, I think. These are days that come with two football practices. We either practiced in the morning and again at night or before lunch and again after lunch. They are hard, hard days. The sun beats down, making the air around feel like a sauna. The exercises feel as if they'll never stop and you'll drop dead right there, in the middle of another high-step or running drill. The exhaustion and heat, though, remove any concern you have about dropping dead right there on the field.

At least you'd get to lie down.

Two-A-Days weed out the guys who don't want to do the hard work necessary to be a team football player. They also get the team conditioned and ready for the coming season within the time allotted by the rulebook. For the first three days, we couldn't put on pads. Those are the rules. So, we conditioned. Running. Running some more. Push-ups. Sit-ups. Leg lifts. Jumping jacks. Come up with an aerobic activity, we did it. Coach Farris—assistant coach at the high school—pushed us, then pushed us harder. Head Coach Mike Whitaker did the same.

With our bodies pushed to the breaking point, we received information about new plays and an expectation that we'd quickly memorize them. That's the point of Two-A-Days: take a kid who's been slacking off all summer and turn him into a player that is ready physically and mentally to perform on the field when the lights are blazing, his body's exhausted, and he needs to focus on the play at hand.

I hated it. I hated more that it took me longer to do some things than the other guys. Two-A-Days time is brutal. Going through it blind is worse. Lots of us players throw mental pity parties. No one could possibly understand what we live through to be able to represent them on that field on Friday night. We trudge home each day battered and bruised and trying to remind ourselves that there is a purpose to endurance.

Halfway into Two-A-Days, I melted down.

Dropped off at my house by a teammate's mom, I trudged through the living room and into my bedroom still in full pads. I barely had the energy to take them off, wanting with every fiber of my being to just collapse on the bed—sweat, dirt, and all—and go to sleep. But I couldn't. I needed to clean up. Change clothes.

I took off the pads. They fell to the floor.

Which is a mistake for a blind person because you can't see where things fall, and then you trip over them. I tripped, righted myself, and managed to find the dresser drawer. I pulled out a pair of shorts and shirt.

I felt my way to the bathroom, frustrated and tired with the idea that this part was the easy part for everyone else but still a struggle for me. Feel around, find the faucet. Feel around, get into the shower. Feel around, find the shampoo. Feel around, find the soap. Everything took longer and required more effort and—after days and days of running, lifting, practicing, crawling, tackling, and more—I wanted something as simple as a shower to be easy.

I stood in the shower, letting the water cascade down my back and the frustration mount. Soap. I needed soap. I waved my hand around, seeking the soap dish.

Every.

Single.

Solitary.

Thing.

Is.

Harder.

I finished getting clean. Felt around for the towel. Dried off. Felt around for my clothes. Put them on. Felt my way down the hallway to the living room.

I collapsed onto the couch and allowed the thought that had been niggling at the back of my mind all day to come to the front: I want to quit.

I'd never wanted to quit football. Ever. The idea felt foreign but very enticing. Laying down some of the fight. Some of the difficulty. I had a good excuse. Blindness! Everyone would understand. No one could expect me to keep playing into high school. I'd finished strong, with a middle school championship. Now, I could quit.

Because, really, did I *want* to put this amount of work into football anymore? Did I want to beat up my body, battle my blindness, pull my mind into submission every single day? Did I want to walk back out on that field tomorrow and do it all over again for six hours?

I felt around for the phone and dialed Mom at work.

"Mom, I want to quit."

Neither Mom nor Dad could get home to find out what had gone wrong with me and discuss it. They were alarmed. Never had I wanted to quit . . . well, anything. Quitting isn't a part of my nature. Plodding forward despite the circumstances is my nature.

I get that nature from them.

I slumped on the couch, staring into darkness, allowing the idea of quitting to take shape and form. Life would be easier. No more tripping over equipment. No more relying so much on Mom to not only live her life, but help me live mine. It'd be easier for all of us.

Except that I loved being a Corbin Redhound. I loved the team, the plays, the playing. Did I love it enough to keep going?

Could I keep going? Could Mom? We were pretty near the ends of our ropes. Dad spent every waking moment on the effort to find another job. September 30 bore down on us like a freight train. Mom couldn't leave her position now, not with his layoff in the mix.

There would be no additional help. If anything, the necessitation to help me needed to lessen so that Mom's stress level could decrease.

And the only way I could have any part in making things easier on her and our family was to quit football.

They arrived home that evening at nearly the same time. They found an exhausted, worn out, done kid on the couch.

"It's just too hard," I said.

"Mom's quitting her job and coming home," Dad replied.

"What?"

"We've been talking and praying about it for a while," Dad said.

Mom eased onto the couch beside me and took my hand. "God is being clear with us. It's time for Mom to quit her job and come home full time."

"But you don't have a job in a few months." I didn't want to look this gift horse in the mouth, yet I couldn't understand the logic at play.

"God's being clear, Travis," Mom said. "We follow His lead. Even when it makes no earthly sense."

The wisdom inherent in their obedience soothed my weary soul. I found myself nodding before my thoughts truly caught up to the truth of my affirmation. "Okay."

They hugged me together. "Okay," Dad said.

The enduring oasis in my life is a set of parents who rely on God to be who He says he is and do what He says He'll do. With more peace than is understandable this side of Heaven, Mom gave notice at First National Bank and came home full time.

Knowing she would be there gave me the kick I needed to stick it out. I went back to practice the next day and dug in.

Friends and family questioned the wisdom of Mom quitting her job. They didn't wonder at the need for it—raising a child with blindness is more than a full-time job itself—but they questioned the wisdom of doing so when my dad had already been given notice.

But my parents made the decision in peace. They kept walking forward, trusting God to do and be what He said. Years spent in faithful relationship to Him gave them the assurance of discerning the guidance and Who gave it. They knew their Lord directed this and so they lived among the uncertainty in joy.

Days flew off the calendar, bringing us closer and closer to September 30. Dad's last day at Interstate Coal. My parents never wavered from their decision.

Not even when Dad arose the morning of September 30 and drove to work. No new job lined up. No certainty of the next door that would open, only a calm assurance that it *would* open.

That day, Dad received a call. A job in Corbin had opened up, working for an Atlanta-based company. Would Dad be interested in an interview?

He would.

Dad came home and we all went to my game that night, buoyed by the knowledge that God continued to go before us.

He started his new position on November 1—making more money than he and Mom had ever made together.

In the winter workouts my freshman year, I injured my shoulder. But what's a shoulder injury when I already played blind? This would *not* stop me.

I wore a shoulder brace for my sophomore season, then had surgery that Spring. I never, ever wanted to quit again. Watching my parents walk through their time of testing strengthened my resolve. I'd been born to play football at that moment in time and I knew it. No force on earth could be greater than the certainty of running in His will.

I played center all four years of high school as #63 (#67 wasn't available). Mishaps sputtered to the surface along the way. Our homecoming game freshman year provided one of them.

I hadn't been expecting to play—Coach Whitaker didn't have quite the same commitment to the idea of a blind football player as Coach Farris—so I was surprised when, during the fourth quarter, Coach Farris called out, "Travis, you're getting in."

"Um, okay." I dashed out onto the field toward the sound of my team's voices. A teammate snagged my jersey and pulled me in. I listened to the play being called—a running play to the right—and went to the line with the guys.

We successfully completed the play, and I headed toward where I assumed our huddle would be. Hearing voices, I gathered in—to the wrong team's huddle.

Ever want to experience hostile territory? Insert yourself into the opposing team's huddle in the middle of a football game. They were *not* pleased to see me there and, having no knowledge that I was blind, thought I'd done it on purpose to spy or mess with their heads.

Coach hollered at my teammates from the sidelines. "Get Travis! Somebody get Travis! Guys, you've gotta make sure somebody gets him to the right huddle!" We didn't have to learn that lesson any further. After that, a teammate always made sure I made it to the right team's huddle.

There were other times. Comical times. In another play on a different day, I snapped the ball and moved forward but didn't make contact with my man. "Where's my man? Where's my man?" I called to my teammates.

"I'm over here!" the opponent called out.

Nothing like playing Marco Polo in the middle of a football game.

And yet another comical time: during a JV game against Bell County, an official made a really bad call. I mean, bad enough that fans from both sides were shocked and pretty vocal about it. I hollered, "Hey, ref, you're as blind as I am!" —right about the time the crowd had died down. Our side thought it was hilarious. The opposing team had no idea what I was talking about.

Another comedic moment happened my senior year. By that point, our team worked like a well-oiled machine. Word had spread past Corbin about the blind football player, but since none of us ever made a big deal of it, most opposing teams and their fans had no clue.

I'd gotten to play the entire second half of a game that we ended up winning. After the last play, the official grabbed the ball and tossed it to me. "Here you go, 63."

I turned toward his voice.

The ball hit my chest and landed at my feet.

"What's the matter? Are you blind or something?" he asked.

"As a matter of fact, I am," I said.

He paused. "Wait. You mean to tell me you're completely blind, you played this entire second half, and I didn't know it?"

"That's exactly what I'm telling you," I said, smiled, and walked away.

While I played center for every game, one moment came when Coach Whitaker moved me to a new position for a brief period of time. Senior Year. The Pigskin Classic. Playing against the Lynn Camp Wildcats. I doubted I'd get put in, but Coach decided towards the end of the game to give me some field time.

"Travis? You think you can play defense?"

I shrugged. "Sure."

Coach put me in to play nose tackle. Same spot in the line I usually played, but on the opposite side of the ball. My task was to disrupt the offensive line as soon as the ball was snapped. I needed to take down the man right in front of me, same as always.

The announcer—a Corbin man—noticed that I'd walked

onto the field with the defensive line. He let the crowd know what they were about to see.

I heard the ball scrape the ground and took a giant leap and swing of the arms toward the guy in front of me. The guy stumbled. One of my teammates joined in.

Down he went.

Humor is a big help in getting through the space between oases or walking along with people who don't know how to walk beside a blind man. If I acknowledge the absurdities created by my blindness, it allows them to consider in better detail the life I lead.

For instance, I tell the story of a blind guy who walks into a department store and starts swinging his dog around over his head.

A worried associate scurries over, glances at the poor dog flying through the air, and asks, "Sir, *what* are you doing?"

"Just looking around," he says.

Or I tell them about the time I ran right over an official *during a game*. Poor ref never saw me coming. Which is okay, because I never saw him standing in the way.

If I stay open to it, living the life of a blind man in a sighted world provides a lot of opportunity for laughs, and not just on the football field.

There's the time at youth camp when I walked from the bathroom to the bedroom of my cabin completely naked—with the window wide open. Oops. Sorry, folks. Nothing to see here but a blind guy who doesn't have a clue you're looking at him.

Stellar example of a fine Christian young man.

And then there are times when sincere people forget that I'm blind. I like these moments. They let me know that not everyone sees me as "different."

We all know how much slacking off happens right before Christmas break. Teachers don't want to start a new unit and then break for weeks only to reteach what was forgotten during the holiday. Kids care way more about presents and the break than making sure every i is dotted and t crossed before the final bell rings.

Mrs. Kinsel, my homeroom teacher, had hit on a solution to getting through the final day before Christmas break: class movie time. She told us she had a very special movie prepared.

The room went very silent.

I listened carefully. Strained to hear something, anything, so I could guess at what everyone was seeing.

Finally, a full two minutes into the silence, I raised my hand. "Mrs. Kinsel?"

"Yes, Travis?"

"When are you going to start the movie?"

Laughter rang out as I heard Mrs. Kinsel groan. "Oh no! I have not done this!"

She'd chosen a "very special" movie all right.

A silent film.

Through all the absurdities and challenges, our little family rolled on. While I didn't have the high school football career we'd envisioned, I *did* have one. And, for nearly all of it, we managed to keep my blindness a secret from the other teams.

Until the football camp before my senior year, that is.

A gentleman in Corbin called WKYT in Lexington and informed them Corbin had a blind football player and a story should be done on it. The segment aired that evening on the news.

A couple of weeks later, Tim Whitmier of the Associated

Press called us. Could he come do a story? We agreed.

He came to town and interviewed us, Coach Farris, and some others. He let me know he would put the story on the AP wire and from there no one could tell what might happen. Every paper in the country could pick it up or not one.

About a week later, we began receiving newspaper clippings from all over the country, including *The New York Times* and *USA Today*.

A journalist with *The Louisville Courier-Journal* called. Could she come to town and do a feature?

"Sure," I said. I hung up the phone and felt my way to the kitchen to inform Mom.

"Oh yeah," Mom responded, "NBC called today. *The Today Show* wants to interview you, too."

Nice little tidbit to mention, Mom.

The media attention set Corbin all abuzz. We'd never seen anything like it. I received letters and calls from across the nation, including entire classrooms of third- or fourth-grade students. I had all of them read to me.

I wouldn't have had any of that experience, had I kept my sight.

And I highly doubt I would have gotten the call that determined my next step: college.

8

RUNNING THE RACE BEFORE YOU

WHAT'S THE #1 THING ON EVERY HIGH SCHOOL SENIOR'S mind?

It's nearly over.

What's the #1 thing on every high school senior's parent's mind?

College.

Could I live away from home? Sure. A mobility instructor would come back into the picture whenever I decided where I'd be. Together, we'd explore a new campus, learning how to navigate sidewalks in order to get to classes and my dorm room and everywhere else.

Dad, Mom, and I discussed the probability that Georgetown College in Georgetown, Kentucky would be suitable. At just one hundred miles from home, it allowed for independence but remained close enough to my family. Scholarship money awaited me if I enrolled.

But I'm a kid growing up in Kentucky. Any Kentuckian can tell you where I really wanted to go and what I wanted to be next: a University of Kentucky Wildcat.

I arrived home from school one day to find Dad and Mom with exciting news. The media coverage from *The Today Show* had been viewed at UK. They'd called and invited us to the unofficial recruit gathering at Senior Day.

Unofficial recruit invitations are just that. Kind of a

get-to-know-you, see each other in person and figure out if there's potential for a future together thing. No commitments are on the table. No promises. No offers. Just an invitation to observe the team and facilities, meet some people, and determine if you're interested.

As if anyone is going to visit the University of Kentucky and not be interested.

I invited my fellow Redhound, Derek Neal, to join us for the visit. We arrived at Nutter Field House and fell into line with all the other unofficial recruits—seniors from all over. Derek described the enormous building that provided a field for the football team to practice, but also served as the dry-land training facility for the dive and swim teams. It's 132,000 square feet of awesomeness.

We retrieved our game tickets (UK would go head-to-head with Vanderbilt later in the day) and entered the Field House for lunch. They'd set it up on the actual turf field. The Recruiting Coordinator welcomed us warmly and shared the history and dimensions of the building. I wasn't hungry for much of anything besides getting on the actual playing field. Derek and I wolfed down our food amid the cacophony of other seniors doing the same, then told my parents we'd meet them in the stands later and headed for the tunnel that emptied onto . . .

. . . bliss. Commonwealth Stadium. Home of the Kentucky Wildcats football games.

Commonwealth Stadium is even more enormous than the Field House. Derek kept up his descriptions as we emerged from the tunnel onto the field. Stands rise on all four sides, creating a bowl of people – every single one of which has a direct line of sight to the game. Over 67,000 people can be seated at any time and, today, they would be.

The huffs and movement of the team rose around me.

"They're prepping," Derek said.

I could picture them lying down and stretching out. College warriors preparing for battle while high school seniors roamed among them, contemplating whether this would be the home for their future conquests.

"Hey, there's Coach," Derek said. "Come on, let's go meet him."

Sure let's also grab lunch with the President and the Pope while we're at it.

Coach Hal Mumme. Co-founder of the air raid offense. A legend in Kentucky. Head coach. Derek grabbed my arm and pulled us toward where I assumed Coach Mumme stood.

"He's turning toward us," Derek whispered.

"Oh, hey, Travis! How ya doing?"

He knew me on sight? Hello, surreal land.

"Great! Thanks so much for having us."

"Our pleasure. I saw your piece on *The Today Show.* Hope you're enjoying your visit."

"We are."

"So, listen. I really want you to come and be a part of our program, work on our equipment staff. I think you could add a lot to our team. We'd make sure your tuition and stuff is covered. Sound good?"

"Yes."

Oh my goodness, absolutely, all the way, where do I sign up, *yes.*

As soon as we got back from Lexington, Mom and I began filling out the application for UK. The final months of my senior year ticked by as I waited. Could they deny me even with Coach Mumme's offer? Would they?

Each day, I walked to the mail box and felt inside. Some days there were letters that felt like the right size. I took those to

Mom, but within seconds she' tell me they were bills or credit card offers.

Nothing from UK.

Then, finally, I handed Mom the stack of the day's mail. "There's one from UK!" she announced.

My acceptance letter. Right there, sitting in Mom's hand. "We are pleased to inform you," she read . . .

Now, about that equipment position, Coach. How do we make that official?

I didn't quite know how to take the next step. Dad, Mom, and I discussed it and decided to wait a bit. Maybe the next move would come from the Coach, too.

That March, I sat in Coach Johnny Crawford's Criminal Justice class, telling myself to pay attention and not slack off just because the year happened to be coming to a close. Even with the media attention that had plastered my story all over the country for a few days, I felt very thankful to still be—in Corbin—just plain old Travis Freeman. Just as with that first day on the field with Coach Farris, no one treated me much different than any other kid.

Laughter and conversation swirled around me. Then, the classroom phone rang.

Coach Crawford did *not* appreciate being interrupted in class. He sighed loudly and answered the phone. Then I heard, "Travis, phone call!"

My stomach plummeted. It had to be bad for them to patch a call through and interrupt Coach Crawford.

I stood and started toward the front of the room.

"Everybody else, shut up!" Coach Crawford continued as I walked. "It's Hal Mumme!"

I froze. What did he just say? I shook my head, made it to

the front of the room, and held out my hand. Coach Crawford placed the phone in it.

"Hello?"

"Travis, this is Hal Mumme."

"Yessir. Hello." Didn't I just sound brilliant?

"I thought I'd call and make it official. You still interested in being an equipment manager for us?"

"Yessir."

"Good, good. We'll get you up here for a spring practice, let you meet the team."

The rest of the class time fell victim to Hal Mumme stories and what-ifs about my future.

Now I just needed to figure out how to get around a brand new environment, what I wanted to major in, where everything in my new dorm building lay . . . and, oh yeah, how to be an equipment manager for a major university's football program.

I couldn't wait.

We called the Kentucky Department for the Blind (DFB) and requested a mobility instructor to work with me on getting around campus. During the summer between high school graduation and first college semester, I met Kim on campus several times.

At first, Kim thought things would be easy. "There's a bus that runs from right outside your dorm over to the main campus," she said. "You just need to catch the bus."

"I don't want to rely on the bus," I replied. "I want to know how to get around on my own."

"Oh."

I waited through her pause.

"Okay, we can do that."

And off we went, meandering down sidewalks, around

corners, beside benches and trash cans and plants. Just like when
I learned to snap a ball, the name of the game was repetition.

Walk from dorm to first class holding on to Kim's arm.

Walk from dorm to first class with Kim behind me, offering instruction.

Walk from dorm to first class with Kim behind me, silently
watching, ready if I misstepped.

Do it again.

And again.

And again.

We did this for every single place I needed to be on campus.
As we walked, I formed a grid in my mind of the location of
buildings, classes within those buildings, and pathways between
them.

Finally, moving day dawned. Dad, Mom, and I packed up my
clothes and set off on the same highway that had taken me back
and forth to the hospital. Lexington, here we come.

I'd been provided with a room in the Kirwan-Blanding Complex. It's on the south campus, at the corner of University Drive
and Complex Drive. There are two tall towers with four low-
rises around each tower, poking out like spokes. My room on
the first floor awaited me.

I'd been assigned a roommate—fellow Corbin Redhound
Josh Baker. Josh would prove very helpful, as he'd already been
on campus for a year and knew his way around. Another friend,
Robbie Taylor, moved in to a room on the floor above me. He'd
spent his first college year at University of North Carolina Ashe-
ville, and decided to come home to Kentucky.

Because of my involvement with the football program, I
needed to arrive on campus two weeks early. My parents and
I settled my stuff into my side of the room, and I kissed and

hugged them goodbye. Time to see if I could make it on my own.

I'd already landed on the idea of a major in business administration for two reasons: I love business, and—perhaps more importantly—the major didn't require any foreign language classes.

My first morning, I woke up energized. I rehearsed in my mind the path to the Nutter Training Center and set off. The Training Center is a different building than the Field House. It's over 48,000 square feet of space that includes two grass fields and a turf field, all with stadium lighting.

I arrived at the Nutter Center and found my way to the office of my new boss, Tom Kalinowski, whom I'd met with over the summer. Coach Mumme had shared with Tom two pieces of information:

He'd brought me on board to be an equipment manager.

He'd done so despite the fact that I was blind.

Tom shook my hand, then asked me to sit down and talk a second.

"I have no idea how this is going to work," he informed me. "But Coach Mumme says it's going to work, so you and I are going to make it work."

I could only grin. Coach Farris would love this story.

"Yessir, I'm ready."

Thankfully, Tom had the place very organized. Every piece of equipment nested in its proper place. As soon as I learned what belonged where, I could be helpful in retrieving or returning things to their correct location. I also became an expert at folding towels, game pants, game jerseys, and practice pants.

It took time in the beginning to learn the routine of practice on the field. As soon as I understood what happened and when, I could help with drills by holding the chains; and on days it rained, I could dry footballs for practice.

On one day after practice in Commonwealth, we managers

loaded up a golf cart with all of the equipment we had used during practice. One of the other managers had the idea that I could drive the golf cart back to Nutter. So I did.

I could hear Coach Mumme's voice getting closer as we drove out of the stadium. When I realized we were passing him, I said, "Hey, Coach!"

"Hey, Travis!" he said normally. Then he must have looked up. "Travis?!"

We all laughed and just kept going.

By the end of the first season, Tom and I had not only made it work but found a way to enjoy the process together. I think he liked joking around with me to relieve the stress of the job. I loved every single minute of it, for five full seasons.

Okay, not *every* single minute. There were tough times as well—like when the team traveled.

I function fairly well in familiar space and inside a routine or pattern. Traveling takes away both of those things. And when that happens, I'm ripe for an accident.

Such as the time we went to Bloomington, Indiana, to play the University of Indiana. The managers had been assigned to housing quarters in the form of townhouses. I entered the townhouse and felt my way up the wooden banister, counting steps and trying to form a map in my mind. Some step configurations are easier than others. These were not the easy ones. Up a flight, turn, up a triangular step, shuffle forward, up two more smaller steps, encounter the hallway.

Got all that?

I thought I did as well until I attempted to come down them. I missed the triangular second step and went flying—teeth first—into the wooden banister. Two of my teeth shattered on impact, leaving my nerves exposed. And let me just say, that is *horrifically* painful. At first, I tried to tough it out. We cleaned up the blood, I took Tylenol, and determined to wait until the end of the trip to go to the dentist.

Did I mention the part about two exposed nerves? Pain seared through my head with every breath. The next day, one of our bus drivers drove me to Louisville to meet my parents. They picked me up and took me to the dentist in Corbin, but they didn't call ahead to tell him of the damage he'd encounter in my mouth.

The dentist came around the door of the exam room already greeting me. "Travis! How are you—oh my gosh, what have you done?"

It took two root implants, two crowns, and twenty thousand in dental work to put me back together again.

Which isn't to say that I didn't have some challenges to overcome on my home campus, too. The first day of classes, I rose, got dressed, and confidently headed away from my dorm toward the location of my Thursday 8 a.m. class.

I navigated to a seat and had just settled in when the teacher greeted the class with, "This is Japanese Culture 110."

Oops.

Um.

Hmm.

Gathering up my stuff, I stood and walked outside. What had I done?

I backtracked through the mental map I'd formed. Did I turn too soon? Too late? Miss a sidewalk? And then it dawned on me.

I'd just walked to the location of my Tuesday 2 p.m. class. On a Thursday morning.

Oh, well. Guess we could call that another trial run for Tuesday.

The thing is, everyone has challenges, they're just different from mine most of the time. I might have a hard time getting from point A to point B, but so do a lot of people without Google Maps. Goodness, I have a friend who has trouble even *with* the use of Google Maps.

I'm not the first guy to miss a step and fall down the stairs or need to figure out a pattern before I can ease into being useful.

We're all wandering around in this desert of a broken planet, trying to find our way to the next oasis. Most of the time, I'm afforded a little more grace on the journey because I'm making my way in the literal dark. What could happen, though, if we granted each other a little more grace automatically? What if we realized that everyone, in at least one sense or another, is walking in the dark? Would we be quicker to reach out with a helping hand instead of a pointing finger?

I like to think so.

After five seasons at UK, I earned my Bachelor's in Business Administration in December 2003 and set my sights toward Southern Baptist Theological Seminary. Time to learn more pathways to classrooms and form new pathways in my mind and soul.

Time to go from ballgames to Bible lessons.

I am fascinated by the Bible. It is the only history book that weaves together stories and families over thousands of years into a breathtaking tapestry of redemption and restoration of mankind to God. It is full of hope and joy for us. It is a marvel of literary masterpiece, incorporating poetry and prose, history and prophecy. There is no other book of its caliber on the planet.

For my first semester at SBTS, I lived in Lexington and commuted with a friend who had also enrolled in seminary. After the first spring semester, he decided seminary didn't serve as the next right step and dropped out.

So in the summer of 2004, I found an apartment on campus and moved to Louisville. As with my stay at UK, a mobility expert joined me early on the SBTS campus to learn sidewalks and classroom locations.

My first two years of seminary don't demand much space here. I knew a lot of people, but didn't form deep friendships with any of them. I think everyone assumed everyone else already had true friendships; therefore little effort was made to continue growing new ones. At least in my case, the assumption didn't bear out.

Not that much time could be devoted to anything besides studying, anyway. I studied more in my first semester of seminary than I had the entire time I spent at UK. The instruction poured over me in class and I struggled to take it all in. New ways of thinking. New methods of reading. New ideas. Good ideas that pushed my brain to think critically and analyze carefully.

While I buckled down and focused on studies, a group of about eight guys moved into a house just off campus. One of the guys, Jason Dees, also served as a pastor at a small church down in southern Indiana. He commuted back and forth, preaching on the weekends and attending seminary during the week. On one of his drives home, he saw a sign that read, "Pet Ducks and Geese for Sale."

He must have been exhausted. Because, come on, who stops for that kind of sign?

This guy. He stopped and bought one duck and one goose, put them in his car, and brought them back to the house he shared with seven other guys.

The duck and goose went to live in the backyard.

The duck died. Do not ask me why. I wasn't there. I had my head deep into my books. I saw nothing. (I never do!)

Left without his duck compatriot, the goose wandered around looking lonely. So the guys decided to return him to a goose family. They bundled the goose into a car and drove it over to Cherokee Park, where they introduced it to the goose family living on the pond in the park.

The goose didn't get it. As soon as the guys walked away, he clambered out of the water and waddled along behind them.

Again, the guys shooed the goose into the water. Again, they walked away. Again, the goose followed.

He might have been slow, but eventually the goose caught on and stayed in the water. The guys watched as he moseyed over to the other geese and received a warm welcome of flapping feathers and friendly honks.

This is the kind of story I heard when I fell in with the guys from The Duck and Goose House. Aside from their questionable choice of pets, they were—and remain—an incredible group of godly men. We established a routine of Sunday night prayer and Monday night dinner. Each Sunday night, ten or so of us gathered in the living room to talk about the previous week, the upcoming week, and where we needed prayer. We held each other accountable. We shared freely and leaned on each other as we embarked on real adulthood together as Christian men.

On Monday nights, one guy made dinner for all the rest. Sometimes a professor and his wife joined us. Other times, it remained just us at the table, laughing and sharing and reveling in the friendship in our little oasis.

We didn't always stay at the house, though. One night, somebody asked me to tell the group about the last time I drove. Short of that golf cart incident at UK, I had never driven. The guys couldn't believe it, and they weren't about to let it go. The next thing I knew, I was sitting behind the wheel of a Mountaineer and listening to one of the guys describe both how to drive and what lay around us in the empty parking lot.

I eased my foot to the gas and felt the Mountaineer creep forward. Letting my foot fall a bit further, I picked up speed. Soon, we moved along at quite a clip—way too much of a clip for someone who can't even see where he's going.

Listening to the instructions of my friends, I maneuvered the vehicle to the edge of the parking lot, ready to cross the road into another parking lot. I zoomed forward.

"Watch out!" somebody cried.

Oops. We barely missed another car. I wonder what that driver would have thought, had he been hit by a blind driver?

Could I have said he was in my blind side?

We made it safely into the next parking lot and I actually managed to park the Mountaineer in a space right in front of my apartment. Victory!

We went on other adventures, some of which didn't end quite as well as the driving experiment. With Cherokee Park so close at hand and full of hills, the arrival of winter snow could only mean one thing: sledding. And 2009 brought us an opportunity like no other in the form of an enormous ice storm.

Now, I know I've already shared my sledding incident. I'm not dumb. I joined in with the guys for this sledding adventure in a *park*, not on a road. At Dog Hill in Cherokee Park to be exact. Tons of people skied there, packing down the ice and snow for slick runs. No danger of any cars pulling into my lane of adventure. We piled on our sleds and flew down the icy hill, falling off at the bottom and jumping up to do it all over again.

It was nearly impossible to get back up the hill, so much ice coating the path, but we did it. We hopped on for another ride and careened all the way down, unable to hold to any real path because the entire surface of the hill had become one enormous sheet of ice.

We all fell off, grabbed our sleds, and began the trudge back up the hill. Someone got the bright idea that we should take fewer sleds down, then we'd have less to carry back up. So, three of us piled onto one sled, layered on top of each other, and pushed off.

"We're gonna hit them! Lean! Lean!" one guy yelled.

"What?!"

"No, they've moved. Oh no!"

I felt the guys fly off in either direction. Now this was more like it. Flying along solo, holding on for dear life to the edges of the sled.

I grinned, baring my teeth to the frigid air.

WHAM!

I rammed into a tree and stopped on impact. I lifted my head, spitting out tree bark, then dropped it back to the ice.

One of my friends—15 feet away—saw my head fall and just knew I'd died.

"Whoa, dude," said a guy whose breath I could smell even from the ground. "That was the best wreck all day! I so would have bailed out before that."

I listened to the snuff of snow as he walked away. Three of the girls who'd come with us rushed to my side, ready to deploy their expertise as nurses. One took off her glove, packed it with snow, and pressed it to my forehead. Another checked for signs of a concussion and made sure my teeth were still in place.

My phone beeped, and I pressed the button to hear the announcement that Florida State had beaten Duke. "Yes!" I mumbled through my split lip.

One of the girls said, "You're crazy."

I responded, "No, I just don't like Duke."

They managed to get me up and over to our car, then drive me to the hospital. A CT scan revealed my brain still sat in its proper location.

Three stitches, an x-ray, and painkillers for whiplash later, I knew two things: sledding without sight is rough on a guy; and, ironically, I had a sinus infection.

Unlike the one that stole my sight, this sinus infection sat in the usual areas. Antibiotics ran it off easily enough.

I laugh a little when I think about that. I came into the ER with a possible concussion from ramming into a tree that had been hidden from the sight of my fellow sled riders by a group of people standing in front of it. When the people moved, my friends saw the tree and bailed.

I, of course, saw none of that. I went straight into the tree, teeth first.

And learned I had a sinus infection.

Would that infection, if left alone, have migrated to the location of the one that stole my sight? Would it have taken my life? Highly unlikely. But interesting to consider.

We don't know where the little oases will be as we walk along the cracked earth's floor any more than we know the location of all the little cups of water that get us the next few feet.

We do know, though, that they will be there when we need them. We know that because we have a book that reveals the character of the God who created this earth—the earth we then turned inhospitable to life with our choices.

I thanked God for the detection of my sinus infection—a cup of water—and kept walking.

In three and a half years I earned my Master of Divinity Degree. The only idea for the next step that seemed appropriate was to earn a PhD. I applied for and received acceptance to the program.

Dr. Hershael York served as my faculty advisor. In the three courses I took with him and the hours of advice and guidance he offered, my theology and preaching style took form. He guided me down paths of truth, urging me to think critically and test my faith. I chose to focus on Dr. Tim Keller's use of pre-suppositional apologetics in preaching for my dissertation. Between studying Dr. Keller's sermons and learning at the knee of Dr. York, I finished the PhD program a different man from the one who began.

My voice and style as a preacher emerged. I accepted my PhD and asked the Lord about the next step.

Turns out, you're reading a part of it.

9

IN THE DARK, TOGETHER

IWALK AROUND IN THE DARK. I DON'T SEE IMAGES. I DON'T see shadows. Everything is completely void. It bothered my parents when they visited me at college and, upon leaving, I told them to turn the lights off.

No sense wasting the electricity when I don't need light to see. They struggled with leaving me alone in the dark. (I now have an app on my phone that detects whether a light is turned on in a room so I can turn it off.)

But everyone, really, walks around in the dark. I've mentioned it before, but it bears further exploration: no one has all of life figured out. Some of us have met the Creator of Life and accepted His son, Jesus, as our Savior. We have an internal spiritual light that guides us through the darkness of the world and brings joy. A constant against which to measure thoughts and intentions (the Bible) is profoundly liberating for me.

It doesn't, however, set the world to right in front of us.

But even if we have accepted Jesus as Messiah, as God in the flesh who came down and gave Himself for us, we walk around in *earthly* darkness too. As Paul said to the church at Corinth in I Corinthians 13:12, "For now we see as through a glass, darkly; but then face to face: now I know in part; but then shall I know even as also I am known."

We love to be known. My parents are incredible examples of two people who, having spent most of their lives together, *know* each other. Ask Dad to name Mom's favorite anything, and he probably could. Ask Mom to name Dad's strengths or weaknesses, and she'd list the former, then remain silent on the latter so as not to harm him or their relationship. Ask either of them about any part of their lives together, and they'll recall the details as they happened in relationship with each other. When we sat down as a family to write the story of my life, our memories came in terms of how they affected each other and how we held on to each other through the desert.

Still, no matter how many years they spend together on this earth, my parents will never fully know each other in light of their relationship with God. They will never fully know God on this earth. They will know each other enough to love. They know God enough to love Him. But they—like me, like all— see as through a glass darkly.

Like me, my sighted parents have learned to count steps and driveways.

They swing a cane back and forth along the ground as they walk—albeit not a physical one.

They've formed mental maps that get them from Point A to Point B.

Everyone does this, just not in a physical sense.

Take that first idea—counting steps and driveways—in light of an addiction or habit that should be broken. Routine behaviors are hard to curb. We manage to stop them for a few hours, maybe even a few days; and then we go right back to them. We sigh. We may live in the failure for a while, but then we resolve to try again.

And as we once again begin the process of breaking an addiction or bad habit, we count the hours. We count the days. We study the paths of ones who have found victory in this area and we see how far down their path we've come. We see all these things—passing time and alignment with other stories of victory—as mile markers that attest to the ever-increasing nearness of our destination. They are taps of our canes.

I do the same thing, just in a literal sense. When I need to reach a house, I count the number of driveways my cane hits and know that, after a certain number, I should turn to my left or right and continue walking to my destination. When an alcoholic counts thirty days, he marks the milestone and keeps walking. When he counts sixty—when his mental cane taps the edge of the sixty mark—he knows where he is.

Or consider my cane itself. The theory of cane travel that Patty Wheatley taught me requires that I sweep the cane across the path in front of me with every single step. By doing this, I ensure that I will be aware of a barrier in my pathway before my foot or body encounters it. Early in the process of learning how to use a cane, I brought more impatience than understanding to the process. I wanted to run headlong and trust that nothing would dare get in my way.

It only takes running into a pole once to knock home the wisdom of using a cane.

Sighted people use canes of all sorts, too. They apply some type of caution and reach out with hesitation before leaping into the next step. They do this for the same reason I do—they've been hurt before by taking a step without consideration. That hurt feeds into the decision to take another step and, instead of leaping forward that next time, cautiously put a toe down to see if all is well before transferring their weight fully. That's sweeping a cane, testing the ground ahead to ensure it's safe for treading. We put out a fleece and ask God to make it wet, to tell us that next step is His will (and therefore safe) before we take it.

And then there are the mental maps. I do them, and so do sighted people. When I moved to the University of Kentucky and then to The Southern Baptist Theological Seminary, a mobility expert came along to help me form a mental map. I had to learn where the pathways were that would get me from here to there. Careful, methodical work went into the process of forming a grid internally to be able to operate well with the external world.

Sighted people do this in multiple ways, too. They are aware of their own needs and desires for food, clothing, shelter, and relationship. They form mental associations with the "right" grocery store, pharmacy, church, doctor, dentist, and other entities that meet wants and needs. A person thinks, "I need fruit," and his mind zaps along a mental pathway to deliver the source of the solution, "Kroger." (Or Publix or Piggly Wiggly or Walmart or wherever.) The person thinks, "My tooth hurts," and her brain forms a pathway to the dentist.

People form mental maps in relationships as well. We make mental notes—consciously or not—about how the person we love responds to certain words or actions. When my family sits down to dinner, we know how to interact well with each other. If I need a napkin, I ask for one and hold out my hand, knowing that Mom or Dad will place a napkin in my hand. No one has to think, "Travis is holding out his hand and asking for a napkin. Oh, right, that's because he can't see that the napkins are a foot in front of him. Let me tell him that, pick one up, and put it in his hand." No, we have a routine of interacting with each other.

Everyone develops this. Couples develop inside jokes, parents learn the ways to bring about obedience from their children, and friends gain awareness of each other and hold each other accountable. We all form mental pathways in how to navigate the broken space between us. I form them to get to classes on a college campus. Sighted people form them to find navigable pathways in relationship and life.

We're not that different, you and me. We use canes of

different sorts. We make mental maps for navigation. We feel our way through the steps of life.

And while we feel our way through the darkness, walking out life's journey, there are bonfires and candle flames along the way. I can see them, too, and I'll share how.

I was once told a story about John Wesley, founder of the Methodist denomination. I do not know if it is an accurate story, but I do know that the truth within it is. The story goes that someone once asked Mr. Wesley why he thought that his presence drew such large crowds of people. What was it that he brought to a place that drew people? What made people leave their homes and walk or ride—sometimes for days—to gather beneath the sound of his voice?

Wesley responded that all he did was set himself on fire for the Lord. His love for God consumed him, and people came to watch the blaze.

There is profound wisdom in that story. While we bump into each other in the dark, we do occasionally see the welcome glow of something on the horizon. It is always one who has found the Creator of Light and is glowing with the knowledge. We gravitate toward these people not because they are any more whole than we, but because they are a reflection of the perfection that created the world and will one day restore it. Our souls instinctively gravitate to their Maker and reflections of Him.

That is what we do when we see even a reflection of our Heavenly Father's face. I do it, even though I walk in physical darkness. Spiritually, I detect the light just as any believer can. It's why my friendships at the Duck and Goose House mattered so much. My friends there were ablaze with a love of God and a desire to know Him more.

It's why—after years of learning and refinement at

seminary—I sometimes preach today. Despite the darkness that surrounds my physical eyes, I can be a light glowing on someone's spiritually dark horizon. When they arrive at the blaze, I want them to see Him.

While I've learned to recognize how much we have in common— whether sighted or not—in the tools we use to live or the sights and sounds that draw us, I also have learned the importance of community. If we are going to survive in a world darkened by sin and rebellion, then we *must* have community. Community that we are accountable to and that we are responsible for. We need people whose shoulders we can lean on, and at times we need to be that foundation for others.

We cannot make it through the space between oases alone. We need family, friends, and a church that will support us, encourage us, and (if needed) rebuke us. We cannot be afraid of relationships that are intentional and vulnerable.

Because it is only in the vulnerability of relationship that we thrive.

For this reason, God calls us to be His church. All the time, the church looks scarred, broken, and outdated because *we* are scarred, broken, and outdated. But it is also eternal and steadfast. Within *those* descriptors, we form relationships that last for eternity.

When I think of eternal relationships, I think about Derek Redmond. Redmond was an Olympic track athlete from Great Britain who competed in the 400 meter dash of the 1992 Barcelona summer games. He posted the fastest time in the first round and then won his heat in the quarterfinals. In the semifinals, Redmond started well, but as he started down the back stretch he fell to the ground in obvious pain and agony.

Redmond had snapped his hamstring.

As he lay on the track, medical personnel rushed to help him. He shooed them away and struggled to his feet. The entire stadium watched in silence as Redmond began hobbling down the track.

Suddenly, a great commotion arose as a man fought his way down the stands, through security, and onto the track.

Jim Redmond, Derek's father.

Jim wrapped his arm around Derek's waist, and Derek placed his arm around his dad's shoulders. With Derek leaning on his dad, listening to the words of encouragement, the father and son made it all the way to the finish line.

We all need a Jim Redmond in our lives. Someone who picks us up when we fall, wraps an arm around us, and helps get us to the finish line.

For believers, that is the church.

And, finally, this blind man has learned the crucial element to finishing our desert journey: focus. In Mark 4:35-41, there is an account of Jesus and his disciples caught out in a storm on the Sea of Galilee. The waves were breaking over the boat, and the boat dangerously listed from side to side, nearly swamped with each successive toss.

Yet Jesus slept soundly on a cushion in the stern.

The terrified disciples awakened him and demanded, "Teacher do you not care that we are going to die?"

Their words revealed their focus. They were focused on their circumstances, and those circumstances didn't align with what they thought they knew of God. They assumed that because they were in the storm, they would soon die. And because Jesus showed no apparent concern about that approaching outcome, God did not care for them.

They had the wrong focus. Their focus was on their

circumstances, and not on the Man who floated in the boat along-side them.

As difficult as it is, we must look beyond our circumstances to the One who enters into those circumstances with us. We must preach the truth of the Gospel to *ourselves*. The truth that God is good, that He is in control, and that He has our best interests in mind.

And when we are in our darkest days, we must, must, must look to the cross and find in it God's truest expression of love for us. When we see the cross, we can have confidence that God cares for us, no matter what our circumstances indicate.

Do not allow circumstance to tell you about God. Let God tell you what to think of your circumstance.

One final thought. As I write these words, unable to see them form on the screen in front of me, I feel pressed to grow an awareness of the truth that God always has a purpose for our suffering. We may not ever know what that purpose is, but we can be confident that it exists. Job was not given the purpose for his suffering this side of heaven, but he knows it now. On the other hand, the blind man in John 9 can hear Jesus tell his disciples that his blindness existed in order for God to be glorified. He heard the purpose for his ailment!

In every situation and circumstance, God is going to be glorified. That's the crazy thing about this world we live in. God designed it so that He will receive maximum glory. Even in its broken state, it groans along with an unending drive to fulfill its purpose: glorify its Creator.

And that's exactly how we should want it to be.

Because He is the only One worthy of all glory and worship.

And a world that does not strive to bring God maximum glory is not a world worth living in.

10

HOW TO KEEP YOUR MIND
AROUND THE BLIND

IT'S A DARK DESERT OUT HERE, BUT WE HAVE RESPITE. WE can look up and see the stars twinkling and know that they reflect the brilliance of their Maker. Or we can return our gaze here, to our sojourn, where relationships pour refreshing water into our lives. Where communities clear away the hazy waves of heat and point with clarity toward our destination.

I would not—could not—be this far on my journey without the gifts of relationship and community. The woman who wrote a screenplay inspired by my life story is from Corbin. She's part of my community and always will be though she now lives far away. The scholarships I received for school came about because a man in my community called a news station and tipped them off to the story of a blind kid playing football. The football experience I enjoyed is due to the relationship of a gifted and talented mentor, Coach Farris.

Relationships and community give us the refreshment and nourishment to make it another step, another mile.

But for a blind person, relationships come with additional landmines. Situations can be awkward that are second nature for sighted people. Word choices for conversation become over-thought and overwrought, resulting in a stilted back-and-forth that doesn't end up communicating much besides difficulty.

My feet have walked in a physical darkness for two-thirds of my life. This portion of the journey gave me time to amass a short list of the DOs and DON'Ts I wish sighted people knew before they attempted to interact with a blind person. Now, because of the opportunities afforded me through my relationships and community, I have a chance to share those DOs and DON'Ts here. These tips and tricks will help you engage with a blind person, but not lose your mind (or make him want to lose his) in the process.

THE DOs

1. Do talk directly to the person. For a while, I wondered if I disappeared under a cloaking device each time I walked into a restaurant. Servers almost never ask me what I'd like to order, directing their attention and words to a sighted person at the table instead. I'm right there. I can speak. I know what I want. Just ask.

There are allowances to be made for blind people in a restaurant, though. During one restaurant visit, the server arrived with my salad and stopped on the opposite side of the table from my chair. He held out my salad.

Having zero idea of this, I did not respond.

He waved the salad back and forth, trying hard to get it into my line of sight. Yeah, I don't *have* a line of sight.

Finally, a friend at the table noted the dancing salad and grabbed the plate. "He's blind," my friend explained.

The poor server gushed apologies, which—in typical fashion—made me feel horrendous.

I want people to treat me normally, but I do not want them to feel bad when they do not realize I am blind.

Occasionally, a server realizes this from the beginning. The server then treats me like any other customer and even goes that "extra mile" to tell me where things sit on the table and in relation to me. These servers always make a visit to a restaurant more enjoyable.

2. Do ask if you don't know what to do or how to be. Don't think of disability as the big white elephant in the room. It's right there. Ask us how we'd like you to act. We're happy to tell you.

If you ask and we say that we do not need assistance, don't assume that you know better and go ahead and help. If we need your help when you offer it, we will tell you what we need.

Multiple times someone has asked me if I need assistance crossing a driveway or street. When I say, "No, thank you," the person proceeds to grab me by the elbow and try and help me across the space.

Few things are more frustrating to a person who has a disability than having assistance forced upon them. If we need your help, we will either accept it when you ask, or ask you to help us.

3. Do feel free to use words like "see" in conversation. I do talk about watching TV, going to see a movie, or reading a book. Everyone uses these figures of speech in conversation. When you try to substitute what I am doing in place of the figure of speech (i.e. "Did you listen to that movie?"), it only makes the conversation awkward and forced. People usually struggle to use the right word and end up stumbling over their words. Just ask if I watched that TV show.

Which probably begs the question: *How* do I watch TV or a movie? Someone watches with me and shares what happens in the action parts of the show or movie. The person sits next to me and whispers if we are in public, or speaks normally in the living room, telling me what goes on. If you are with a blind person, offer to be their eyes during a show or movie. You will want to give them a broad understanding of the action. If they want further detail, they'll ask.

4. Do offer your arm to a blind person, then walk as you normally would. You do not need to stick your arm out like a chicken wing. Simply hold your arm relaxed at your side. If you encounter stairs, pause for a moment, then climb. Pause again at the top to indicate the stairs are over. If you need to walk in a single file, put your arm across your lower back for the blind person to walk behind you. There is no need to slow your pace with a blind person.

If by accident the blind person falls or runs into something while walking with you, do not panic, overly apologize, or feel terrible about it. Things like that happen. I encounter this circumstance sometimes, too. I'll get up, dust myself off, and keep on going. It will not have been the first time something like that happened, and it will not be the last.

5. Do guide a blind person's hand to the side of a chair and then step away. The person will seat himself. The same thing applies to getting into a car.

I can remember one time I was getting into a vehicle and a person placed their hands on either side of my hips and tried to help guide me to the seat. It felt extremely awkward, and did not help at all. When approaching a car, simply tap the door next to the handle to let me know its location. Then I can approach the door, find the handle, open it myself, and sit down.

6. Do feel free to describe things that are happening around you, helping the blind person to form a mental image of the activity and environment. I appreciate any description of activity around me. But there is a difference in people who describe things to me because they feel obligated to and people who describe things to me because they appreciate the beauty or complexity of what they see. Allow your emotion to carry your description. It helps me understand what you see, and why you want to describe it. And don't go overboard with this. I do not need to know every detail of everything that happens. During a good conversation, do not interrupt it just to tell me about something unimportant.

7. Do identify yourself when approaching a blind person to talk. If we talk enough times, eventually I will remember your voice, but until that happens, always tell me. There have been times that I've had extended conversations with people and I did not know their identity. This type of interaction places me in an awkward situation. I either ask you who you are and risk offending you because I did not know your identity, or I have to carry on a conversation with someone who I do not know. Do not assume that just because you know who I am that I know who you are.

THE DON'Ts

1. Do not automatically make an exception for the disabled person. Most of us want to be treated like everyone else. Remember when Coach Farris yelled at me to get up? I loved him for it. Disabled people appreciate being treated normally. Do not assume we need your help or explanation or assistance. Remember that it is always better to ask, and not to assume.

2. When you see a blind person walking on a sidewalk or crossing a road, **do not adjust your behavior in any way.** We are trained to successfully navigate the world around us. When you come to a stop, we think the light must have turned red and start crossing. If the guy in the lane beside you takes the right course of action and obeys traffic laws, we will become road pizza.

One time as I walked through a busy neighborhood in Louisville, I came to a corner and stopped to observe the traffic before crossing the street. A car turned left in front of me, then stopped in the middle of the street just past me. The driver then got out of his car and ran over to ask if I needed help.

Common sense seems to leave people when they encounter a person with a disability. Did that individual really think that I would stand on the corner until someone asked if I needed help crossing? Maybe, but if he took a moment and thought, he would realize that does not make sense. If I had to wait on someone to ask, I would never make it anywhere on my own.

In another twist on the odd road behavior, if you see a blind person walking on the side of the road, do not stop driving until the blind person passes. Keep on going normally by the blind person just like you would anyone else.

(I realize that people think they're being courteous, but they really are causing more problems than they're preventing. Stopping the car prevents the blind person from hearing other cars around, including those coming in the other direction. Do not be afraid of just driving on by. I will not step out in front of your car. I can hear your motor and will get out of your way.)

3. When you pass a blind person on the street, **do not blow your horn or roll down your window and yell.** If you want to say something, simply roll your window down and speak normally.

4. Don't offer lift assistance or physical assistance of any kind unless we ask. We're not incapable. I have frequently assisted friends and family in moving. And it never fails that they are amazed that I can lift a box, or get on one end of a piece of furniture and carry it from one place to another. Just because I cannot see something does not mean I cannot carry it.

5. Do not be embarrassed by or apologize for questions that your children might ask. I love children and am always willing to answer their questions. How will they ever learn, if they cannot ask? Do not worry about them asking what my cane is for or why I'm holding on to someone's arm. I am not offended by these questions in the least. Let them ask; let them learn; and let them grow.

6. Do not speak in a louder voice when you are talking with a blind person. It amazes me how many people fall prey to this action. They must think that, because I am blind, I also cannot hear. Talk in a normal voice and at a normal pace. If you raise your voice and slow your pace, you only serve to make the conversation awkward and ineffective.

7. Do not take advantage of a person's blindness to play a prank. There is a difference between possessing a humorous view on life and taking advantage to get a laugh. One time I had a friend who constantly joked that he was going to put a Louisville Cardinal shirt in my closet. We joked about it and had a good laugh—until the day he actually did it. And I was angry. I explained my situation and why it upset me. He apologized, and we are still great friends. We all learned something that day. I learned that joking about my disability can always lead to someone taking it too far, and that I had to be willing to deal with those situations. He learned that there is a line, and you should not cross it.

And we all learned just how much I do not like U of L.

There are numerous other rules and suggestions for engaging with the blind or otherwise disabled. The ones listed above are my particular pet peeves, born of twenty years of walking this desert road, tapping my cane to the right and the left, and hearing the taps of "canes" all around. Of forming my mental maps and recognizing that the sighted around me are doing the same thing. My DOs and DON'Ts come from my experience and desire to continue connecting, continue building relationship and community.

Everyone could create a DOs and DON'Ts list for the best way to interact. Because everyone—every single, solitary broken one of us—is disabled and living in a broken world. I

am disabled. You are disabled.
But our disability does not equal inability
Our disability does not equal inability.
Our disability does not equal inability.
Walk on, broken one.
Even if the lights go out.

WHILE MY PARENTS AND I ARE CLOSE AND I'VE TRIED TO incorporate their experience into the telling of my own, I also wanted to give them a chance to speak for themselves. Without their love and support, my journey would be much darker internally. Below are their responses to the questions I thought others might have.

Did you ever get angry at the doctors who missed Travis's infection? Did you ever think about a malpractice suit?

For both of us at first it was frustration, and a bit of anger, because we couldn't get any relief for Travis. We always thought the doctors that actually treated Travis were competent and did their best to help him. God was in control all along, so nothing they did or didn't do caused Travis to be blind. We talked about it, but never really considered a lawsuit. We did not think that was the right thing for us to do, if we believed in God's will for Travis.

How did your friends and family help you through that difficult time? Did anyone do something special that stood out to you?

Our family and friends were there for us. Early on, they stayed with us and encouraged us in every way. We were overwhelmed with visits, cards and food. I think the greatest thing they did was praying with us and for us! We were surrounded with family, friends, our church and a community that did an amazing number of outstanding things for us and Travis. So many, in fact, that we could not point to any one instance or individual.

How much potential did Travis show in football before he lost his vision?

I (Dad) might not be the best person to ask, but in my opinion, Travis showed potential to be a good high school football player. As a player he was smart, had good technique and he loved the game. I don't think he would have played at the college level, but a good high school career would have been reasonable.

What did you think when coach Farris offered to put Travis on the team?

My (Dad) first thought....Is he serious? My 2nd was Yahoooo! My third was, "When can we get started?" As a dad, I thought it was a dream that ended earlier for me and my son when we were told that he was blind. I had given no thought to him actually playing.

I (Mom) was excited because Travis would be a part of a football program and be with his friends. Did I really think he would actually play, though? Not really!

How did you instill so much strength in your son?

As Christian parents, we believed it our responsibility to teach him to love God, study God's Word and respect others. Also, we gave him the example of working hard and being faithful in our commitments. Mary and I gave him to God as a small child and prayed for him every day, as we still do.

What was the hardest part about learning to care for a child who went blind?

As a mother of a 12 year old son who had just lost his eyesight, I wanted to protect him from everything, to do everything for him and care for him. But God had other ideas! God instilled in me the desire to teach Travis how to live in a sighted world. No one cares for a child like a mother does. God gave us that ability, so I thought. "If I die, who will take care of him?" I wanted the assurance of knowing that, when I die, Travis will be able to care for himself. So, we began the journey and I think the strength comes from leaning how to deal with all the obstacles that we faced.

What resources did you find most helpful in raising Travis?

- A home where dad and mom were careful to love and support one another, while we loved and supported him.
- A great family and friends that supported us and Travis.
- A loving church family that helped us teach him about a relationship with God and others.
- Prayer...lots of prayer!
- An excellent public school system that helped us when we needed it.

Travis has accomplished so much. What are you most proud of?

Earning a Ph.D. was great, playing football again was a dream come true, but we are most proud of the confident, but humble, Godly man he has become. We are proud of his relationship with Jesus, of his daily walk with the Lord. When Travis first learned he was blind, he said, "I believe I will see again, but if I don't, I can't wait to see what God's going to do with my life". We are now starting to see the results of that attitude and commitment.

What advice would you give to other parents and caregivers of disabled children?

- Take your difficult situation one day at a time. When you worry about what's going to happen tomorrow, or next week or next year, you become overwhelmed and discouraged.
- Love, but don't smother the child. Encourage, even push the child to get involved in the mainstream and take on challenges. The hardest thing as a parent is to let them go and not over protect.
- Trust that God is in control. He loves your child even more than you do! Pray and seek His guidance for your child.

THESE RECENT DAYS HAVE ADDED ANOTHER DESCRIPTOR to my identity to go along with the ones I shared in chapter one. I'm still blind. Still The Blind Football Player. Still The Christian Blind Professor Who Played Football.

But I am also honored now with the descriptor The Blind Preacher (Who, Yeah, Happened to Play Football). Having an opportunity to share more about the God who sees me through, who lights my way, is incredible. He is the ultimate reason I have hope. He is why I have life, not just survival. He is the source of my purpose.

He can be the source of yours, too. Read on to find out how.

Living Out God's Purpose
Acts 26:12-23

The search for life's purpose has consumed many people's lives. When a devastating blow comes – say, oh, I don't know, sudden blindness – we can fall into a maelstrom of emotion that swirls around this thought: how can I be worth anything now? How can I have a purpose? Be of value?

We all want to feel like we are living for something, like we are accomplishing something. We need to have a purpose for living. This purpose should be something that pulls us out of bed in the morning, and drives us throughout the day. But, as my life attests, it is a dangerous idea to find that purpose within ourselves. We are breakable creatures.

So what can give us such meaning in life? Is there something that we can all live for that will make us feel valuable and fulfilled? That stands apart from us and our circumstance? That is not affected by the darkness or the desert journey? Yes. And that purpose is God's purpose.

In Acts 26 we read about Paul's defense before Agrippa. Paul had been arrested for causing an uproar and was brought before Festus. This raised a bit of a dilemma for Festus because Paul had Roman citizenship, but also now identified as a citizen of the Jewish people. Under whose authority should he be tried? Festus asked Paul if he'd like to be taken back to Jerusalem for his trial, to be tried by the Jewish people. Paul, however, appealed to Caesar as a Roman citizen, which got him sent to Rome.

As was standard procedure Festus had to send with Paul the charges that were brought against him. He had no charges and for this reason he brought Paul before King Agrippa. King Agrippa desired to hear from Paul, and the text says, "Then Agrippa said to Festus, 'I would like to hear the man myself.' 'Tomorrow,' said he, 'You will hear him (Acts 25:22, ESV)." So on the next day Festus brought Paul to stand before Agrippa.

> [26] So Agrippa said to Paul, "You have permission to speak for yourself." Then Paul stretched out his hand and made his defense:

> [2] "I consider myself fortunate that it is before you, King Agrippa, I am going to make my defense todayagainst all the accusations of the Jews, [3] especially because you are familiar with all the customs andcontroversies of the Jews. Therefore I beg you to listen to me patiently.

> [4] "My manner of life from my youth, spent from the beginning among my own nation and in Jerusalem, is known by all the Jews. [5] They have known for a long time, if they are willing to testify, that according to the strictest party of our religion I have lived as a Pharisee. [6] And now I stand here on trial because of my hope in the promise

made by God to our fathers, [7] to which our twelve
tribes hope to attain, as they earnestly worship
night and day. And for this hope I am accused by
Jews, O king! [8] Why is it thought incredible by
any of you that God raises the dead?

[9] "I myself was convinced that I ought to do
many things in opposing the name of Jesus of
Nazareth. [10] And I did so in Jerusalem. I not only
locked up many of the saints in prison after receiving authorityfrom the chief priests, but when
they were put to death I cast my vote against
them. [11] And I punished them often in all the
synagogues and tried to make them blaspheme,
and in raging fury against them I persecuted
them even to foreign cities.

It is during Paul's defense that we see something about God's
purpose for our lives. In verses 12-23 of chapter 26, Paul begins
to tell of his conversion experience, and God's purpose for him.

[12] "In this connection I journeyed to Damascus
with the authority and commission of the chief
priests. [13] At midday, O king, I saw on the way
a light from heaven, brighter than the sun, that
shone around me and those who journeyed with
me. [14] And when we had all fallen to the ground,
I heard a voice saying to me in the Hebrew language,[a] 'Saul, Saul, why are you persecuting me?
It is hard for you to kick against the goads.' [15] And
I said, 'Who are you, Lord?' And the Lord said, 'I
am Jesus whom you are persecuting. [16] But rise

and stand upon your feet, for I have appeared
to you for this purpose, to appoint you as a ser-
vant and witness to the things in which you have
seen me and to those in which I will appear to
you, [17] delivering you from your people and from
the Gentiles—to whom I am sending you [18] to
open their eyes, so that they may turn from darkness to light and from the power of Satan to God,
that they may receive forgiveness of sins and a
place among those who are sanctified by faith in
me.'

[19] "Therefore, O King Agrippa, I was not disobedient to the heavenly vision, [20] but declared
first to those in Damascus, then in Jerusalem and
throughout all the region of Judea, and also to
the Gentiles, that they should repent and turn to
God, performing deeds in keeping with their re-
pentance. [21] For this reason the Jews seized me in
the temple and tried to kill me. [22] To this day I
have had the help that comes from God, and so I
stand here testifying both to small and great, saying nothing but what the prophets and Moses
said would come to pass: [23] that the Christ must
suffer and that, by being the first to rise from the
dead, he would proclaim light both to our people
and to the Gentiles."

First, we see that if we are going to live out God's purpose for
our lives, we must have an encounter with Christ. Paul tells King
Agrippa that he was traveling to Damascus with the intent of
persecuting and destroying the church there (v. 26:12). But Paul
instead encounters the risen Christ, and he is overwhelmed by

the glory of God. The text says that Paul and his companions were so overcome that they fell to the ground in fear. Then Paul heard a voice saying, "Saul, Saul, why are you persecuting me (v. 14)?" When Paul asks who is this, the voice responds, "I am Jesus whom you are persecuting (v. 15)." For Paul, his encounter with the risen Christ was the beginning of living out God's purpose in his life.

Likewise, if we are going to live out God's purpose, we must have an encounter with Christ. We see this elsewhere in Scripture as well. Whether it's Moses at the burning bush, or Isaiah's vision, all people who have purpose encounter Christ. Our encounter with Christ, however, is very different. We may not have a face-to-face encounter. More often, we encounter Christ through his Word. As we read, meditate, and listen to God's Word, we encounter Christ and are changed forever.

Sadly, many people walk through this world having never encountered Christ. They think they have meaning and purpose, but they are empty and unfulfilled. Why?

Because without an encounter with Christ you can have no true purpose to your life. Without the overwhelming ability of Christ, our disability remains just that.

The Acts 26 passage shows us that, to live out God's purpose in our lives, we must encounter Christ, but also we must know our purpose.

• Have you ever encountered Christ? If so, when? What happened?

_____

_____

_____

_____

_____

_____

_____

- What is one time when you have encountered Christ in his Word?

_____

_____

_____

_____

_____

_____

_____

After Paul falls to his face, and Christ reveals himself, he then tells Paul to stand on his feet. He has revealed himself to Paul for a particular purpose (v. 16). Christ called Paul to be a witness of the things that he had seen. He would not go to his own people (the Jews) but would instead be a witness for Christ among the Gentiles. So, upon Paul's encounter with Christ, God calls him to serve as a missionary, testifying to the light.

We have a tendency at times to lose sight of the primary objective. Even as Christians, we look for purpose all around us and miss the ultimate purpose of our existence. We try to find satisfaction in our jobs or families; in sex or money; in fame or fortune, and we do not realize that God has given all of us a greater purpose. Our purpose is the same as that of the Apostle Paul.

We are called to be a witness to the Light.

Does that mean that we all should sell everything and move to an unreached people group? Not at all. Instead, we should seek to be witnesses in our everyday jobs, if that's where the Lord has placed us. If you are a teacher, then you should be a teacher that witnesses to the Light. If you are a doctor, then you should be a doctor that practices for the glory of the Gospel.

If you run a business, then run your business in a way that honors God. In everything that we do, we should seek to witness to the Light. Even if we walk in the physical darkness of blindness, we are witnesses to the Light.

Our actions, words, and relationships should all point people to Christ. Living out God's purpose in our lives requires encountering Christ and knowing our purpose, but it also involves having a clearly defined purpose.

- How can you be a witness to the Light in your present situation?

_____

_____

_____

_____

_____

_____

_____

_____

- What needs to change in your life in order for you to be a witness to the Light?

_____

_____

_____

_____

_____

_____

_____

_____

Paul goes into detail about his purpose for King Agrippa in verses 18 and 22-23. He tells the king that his purpose is "To open their eyes, so that they may turn from darkness to light and from the power of Satan to God (v. 18)." Paul's purpose is to open the eyes of the Gentiles. He is called to lead them from blindness to sight, from one master to another one. Later, in verses 22-23, Paul goes into further detail. He says that he only speaks the truth that Moses and the prophets had. This truth is the reality that Christ suffered, that he was crucified, and that being the first to rise from the dead, he would proclaim the light.

Because I walk around in physical darkness, I find the references to light and dark in this passage of particular poignancy. The Gentiles are in the dark, and Paul has been given the task of breaking into their darkness with the shining Light of the Gospel. That's a Light I walk by as well. It's a Light I can turn on for others, too.

Just like Paul was called to open the blind eyes of the Gentiles, we are all called to do the same for the people who surround us. People have difficulty receiving the truth about themselves or about their children. They cannot see their darkness. They are blind to their own blindness. People see me and think, "I'm not blind like him," but there are times I want to gently say, "Your soul is more blind than my eyes will ever be."

God sends us into the world to bring Light. We must carry out God's will by talking with people, showing them the beauty of the Gospel. We know that their only hope is to repent and place faith in Christ. That is the Light that can bring a person out of the deepest self-imposed darkness.

How is it that we can open someone's eyes to the truth of Christ? We begin by answering their questions. We spend time engaging and discovering what it is that they talk about. What are their struggles of belief? If we know these areas, then we can help shine the Light on them.

More than anything, we love them. We care for people who are hurting and questioning everything around them. These things take patience and grace.

• What are some things that will cause people to refuse to see their own blindness?

_____

_____

_____

_____

_____

_____

_____

• What are some ways that you can serve people who are questioning God?

_____

_____

_____

_____

_____

_____

_____

Finally, we can live out God's purpose in our lives by facing opposition. In verses 19-21 Paul claims that his success in carrying out his mission has spurred his own countrymen to want to throw him in jail. He defends himself by saying that he is doing what God has called him to do. The irony in this situation is that the one who was persecuting has now become the one who is persecuted.

Persecution is not something that we can escape. We may not all face a life or death-type of persecution, but we are all tempted to compromise our beliefs or face humiliation. Maybe it's a difficult family member or coworker. Maybe it's friends who do not believe the same way. Maybe your beliefs will cost you a promotion or clout in the community. All of these things are types of persecution we should expect.

And then there is self-persecution. This happens anytime that you stand in opposition to the commands of Christ. Anytime you are disobedient you persecute yourself by standing in the way of God carrying out his purpose in your life. Frequently we cannot recognize this behavior in ourselves. That is why we need the church. We need people who can challenge us and correct us when it is needed.

- What outside opposition do you face to carrying out your purpose in the world?

_____

_____

_____

_____

_____

_____

_____

- In what ways do you stand in opposition to yourself?

_____

_____

_____

_____

_____

_____

_____

Without an encounter with Christ, we walk around blind and purposeless. When Christ invades our lives, however, nothing is ever the same again. From that moment forward we have meaning and value for the journey ahead. We have something that satisfies and fulfills. We have something that is both exciting and terrifying.

We have the brilliant light of this knowledge: No matter how dark our circumstances grow, Christ is with us, guiding us and directing us with His purpose in mind. He is our sight. He is our Light.

May you walk in that Light that never goes dark.